Everyman's Poetry

*Everyman, I will go with thee,
and be thy guide*

Andrew Marvell

Selected and edited by GORDON CAMPBELL

University of Leicester

D1512179

EVERYMAN

J. M. Dent · London

Introduction and other critical apparatus
© J. M. Dent 1997

All rights reserved

J. M. Dent
Orion Publishing Group
Orion House
5 Upper St Martin's Lane,
London WC2H 9EA

Typeset by Deltatype Ltd, Birkenhead, Merseyside
Printed in Great Britain by
The Guernsey Press Co. Ltd, Guernsey, C.I.

This book if bound as a paperback is subject to the
condition that it may not be issued on loan or otherwise
except in its original binding.

British Library Cataloguing-in-Publication
Data is available upon request.

ISBN 0 460 87812 3

Contents

Note on the Author and Editor

ANDREW MARVELL was born at Winestead, near Hull, the son of a clergyman. He was educated at Hull Grammar School and Trinity College, Cambridge. He travelled on the Continent for four years, and in 1650 became tutor to Lord Fairfax's daughter Mary at Nun Appleton, near York. Many of Marvell's most famous lyric poems seem to have been written at Nun Appleton. In 1657 Marvell became John Milton's assistant in the Latin Secretariat of the Council of State. He was Member of Parliament for Hull from 1659 until his death in 1678.

GORDON CAMPBELL is Professor of Renaissance Literature at the University of Leicester, and President of the English Association. He has written widely on English Renaissance literature, and has also published editions of Ben Jonson and John Milton. He is editor of the interdisciplinary journal *Renaissance Studies*.

Chronology of Marvell's Life

Year	Age	Life
1621		Born 31 March at Winestead-in-Holderness, Yorks, to Revd Andrew Marvell and his wife Anne
1624	3	Marvell family moves to Hull on appointment of Revd Andrew Marvell to a lectureship at Holy Trinity Church
1633	12	Leaves Hull Grammar School for Trinity College Cambridge
1637	16	First poem published (in Latin and Greek) in a Cambridge anthology in celebration of the birth of a daughter to King Charles and Queen Henrietta Maria
1638	17	(April) Mother dies; (November) Father remarries
1639	18	Receives BA. Converts (briefly) to Roman Catholicism, runs away to London, where his father finds him and returns him to Cambridge

Chronology of his Times

Year	Cultural Context	Historical Events
1622		Virginia settlers massacred
1623	Shakespeare 'First Folio'	
1625		Charles I crowned
1626	Bacon, *New Atlantis*	
1627		Anglo-French War
1628	Harvey, 'Circulation of the Blood'	
1629		Charles dissolves parliament (–1640)
1632	Shakespeare 'Second Folio'	
1633	Donne, *Poems*; Herbert, *The Temple*	Laud becomes archbishop (–1645)
1634	Oberammergau passion play performed	
1636		Harvard College founded
1637	Corneille, *Le Cid* performed	
1639		First Bishops' War
1640	Carew, *Poems*	Second Bishops' War; Long Parliament (–1653) Irish rebellion

Year	Age	Life
1641	20	Father drowned crossing the Humber; Marvell abandons MA course
1642	21	Travels in Holland, France, Italy and Spain until 1647 or 1648
1645	24	Visits Richard Flecknoe in Rome during Lent 1645 or 1646 and subsequently writes 'Flecknoe, an English Priest at Rome'
1648	27	Writes 'To his Noble Friend Mr Richard Lovelace' (January?) and, if it is his, the anti-parliamentarian 'Elegy upon the Death of My Lord Francis Villiers'
1649	28	Writes 'Upon the Death of the Lord Hastings'
1650	29	Moves to Appleton House, the Yorkshire home of the Fairfax family, as tutor to Mary Fairfax. Writes 'An Horatian Ode upon Cromwell's Return from Ireland' (summer) and 'Tom May's Death' (December)
1653	32	Recommended by Milton (unsuccessfully) for post in Council of State. Becomes tutor to William Dutton, a young member of Cromwell's circle. Moves to John Oxenbridge's house at Eton
1656	35	In Saumur, a Protestant town in France, with William Dutton
1657	36	Writes 'On the Victory obtained by Blake' (summer). Appointed to the Secretariat of the Council of State
1658	37	Writes 'A Poem upon the Death of His Late Highness the Lord Protector' (September)
1659	38	Elected MP for Hull (and remains an MP for the rest of his life)
1662	41	Spends eleven months in 1662–3 in Holland as diplomat and spy

Year	Cultural Context	Historical Events
1642	Browne, *Religio Medici*	English Civil War (–1649); Tasman lands in New Zealand
1643		Louis XIV crowned (–1715)
1644		Ch'ing dynasty (–1912)
1645	Milton, *Poems*	
1646	Vaughan, *Poems*	
1647		Execution of Archbishop Laud
1648		First Fronde (–1649)
1649		Execution of Charles I
1650	Anne Bradstreet, *Tenth Muse*	
1651	Hobbes, *Leviathan*	Second Fronde (–1653)
1652		First Anglo-Dutch War (–1654)
1653	Walton, *Complete Angler*	Taj Mahal completed
1655		English capture Jamaica
1656		Bernini completes St Peter's (Rome); Anglo-Spanish War (–1649)
1658		Death of Cromwell
1660		Restoration of Charles II
1661		English acquire Bombay
1662		Dunkirk sold to France

Year	Age	Life
1663	42	Travels on embassy to Russia, Sweden and Denmark as Secretary to Earl of Carlisle
1665	44	Returns to England (January)
1667	46	Writes 'Last Instructions to a Painter'
1669	48	Writes 'The Loyal Scot'
1671	50	Submits Latin epigrams in a competition for an inscription on the Louvre
1672	51	Publishes 'The Rehearsal Transprosed' anonymously
1673	52	Publishes 'The Rehearsal Transprosed, The Second Part' under his name. Works as 'Mr Thomas' with Dutch secret agents in England
1674	53	Writes 'On Mr Milton's Paradise Lost'
1677	56	Publishes 'An Account of the Growth of Popery' anonymously
1678	57	Elected younger warden of Trinity House, London. Dies 16 August of a malarial fever
1681		*Miscellaneous Poems* published by 'Mary Marvell'

Year	Cultural Context	Historical Events
1664		British capture New Amsterdam
1665		Great Plague; second Dutch War (−1667)
1666	Bunyan, *Grace Abounding to the Chief of Sinners*	Fire of London
1667	Milton, *Paradise Lost, a Poem in Two Books*	
1669	Racine, *Britannicus* performed	
1670	Racine, *Bérénice* performed	Hudson's Bay Company incorporated
1671	Milton, *Paradise Regained* and *Samson Agonistes*	
1672		Third Dutch War (−1674)
1673		Test Act passed
1674	Milton, *Paradise Lost, a Poem in Twelve Books*	
1678		'Popish Plot' devised by Titus Oates

Introduction

Andrew Marvell is a twentieth-century poet. This may seem an odd
claim for a poet who lived in the seventeenth century, but during
his lifetime Marvell was known primarily as a satirist whose chosen
medium was prose. His poems were published three years after his
death, but there is little evidence that they were widely read. There
are few allusions to Marvell's lyrics in the eighteenth and
nineteenth centuries, though a few were reprinted in collections
such as George Gilfillan's *Specimens of the Less Known British Poets*
(1860). Palgrave, acting on Tennyson's advice, included 'An
Horatian Ode', 'Bermudas' and 'The Garden' in his *Golden Treasury*
(1861), but as late as 1900 a contributor to *Gentleman's Magazine*
could refer to Marvell as a 'forgotten poet'.

The rediscovery of Marvell was, perhaps improbably, occasioned
by the tercentenary of his birth in 1921. T. S. Eliot, in an essay first
printed in the *Times Literary Supplement* in 1921, announced in his
Olympian manner that 'the tercentenary of the former member for
Hull deserves not only the celebration proposed by that favoured
borough, but a little serious reflection upon his writing'. The
serious reflection contained in this essay achieved what Eliot
described as 'the great, the perennial task of criticism', which was
'to bring the poet back to life'. Marvell now lives, and poems such as
'To his Coy Mistress' and 'The Garden' and 'On a Drop of Dew' are
familiar to all readers of English poetry. These poems embody the
classical virtues of elegance and poise, and in their diction reveal
the essence of Marvell's genius to be an incomparable control of
tone and wit and emotional intensity. The origins of the discipline
that achieves the balletic poise of Marvell's poems may lie in his
practice of composition. Both 'The Garden' and 'On a Drop of
Dew' survive in Latin versions that seem to precede the English
poems. Samuel Beckett disciplined his dramatic prose by writing his
plays in French and then translating them into English, and the
existence of these Latin poems (which may be the only survivors of
a larger group) suggests that Marvell may have used the same

technique of composing in an acquired language and then translating into his native English.

The accessibility of the language of Marvell's poems seems to belie the complexity of their tone and substance. One of the most memorably forbidding formulations of the tercentenary celebrations was a comment in *The Bookman* to the effect that Marvell 'expressed into poetry a philosophy as large as that which Coleridge could not reduce into prose. He was a singing Cambridge Platonist.' An analogy with the prodigious learning of Coleridge and the overburdened learned prose of seventeenth-century philosophers may seem inept as well as uninviting, but it points to an important feature of Marvell's poetry, which is that its simplicity is a studied effect and that complex ideas are sometimes conveyed in simple words. He brings to the conventional materials of lyric a mind that is alert and disciplined and a voice that is ironic and oblique. A simple poem such as 'The Nymph Complaining for the Death of her Fawn', for example, is charged by recollections of ancient poems such as Ovid's lament for his lover's parrot and Catullus's for his lover's sparrow and by an implied emotional analogy between grief for a dead pet and sorrow for a departed lover; similarly, the apparent timelessness of the poem is deftly qualified by Marvell's choice of the word 'troopers' in the opening line, because the term was associated with the army of Scottish covenanters who had invaded England in 1640.

The political turmoil of the mid seventeenth century is inevitably reflected in the poetry of the period: no one, least of all a poet, is indifferent to war and revolution. Marvell's own political position is usually not as simple as his critics might hope: to ask whether Marvell's sympathies lie with Oliver Cromwell or King Charles in 'An Horatian Ode', or whether he approved of Fairfax's retirement from the political arena in 'Upon Appleton House', is to invite answers so simple that they could not possibly be true. It is certainly the case that Marvell gradually adopted a form of republicanism that was to take root in France and America (though not, alas, in England), but it would be unnecessarily reductive to use his nascent republicanism as a gloss on poems written in the early 1650s, when the world in which he had grown up had been swept aside by the tumultuous events of the previous decade. Just as Horace's 'Actium Ode' (I. 37) turns from the celebration of Octavian's victory to portray the nobility of the defeated Cleopatra's death, so Marvell's 'Horatian Ode' at once acknowledges the dignity with which the king met his tragic end and celebrates the hopes embodied in Oliver Cromwell as the champion of the new Commonwealth. The intertwining of Marvell's ode with Horace's complicates the matter still further, because the victory celebrated by Horace heralded the death of the Roman republic, for Octavian became (as Augustus Caesar) the founder of a new empire, whereas the execution of Charles signalled the birth of the English republic. The difficulty for the modern reader is not so much the poised ambiguity of Marvell's depiction of the protagonists as the assumption that the violent subjugation of Ireland is a cause for celebration: far from being 'in one year tamed', Ireland continued to smoulder, and the massacres at Drogheda and Wexford over which Cromwell presided still provide fuel for the IRA.

The Romantic poets of the early nineteenth century used poetry as a vehicle for autobiography, and since that time students of poetry have become accustomed to the idea of looking in poetry for an account of the feelings of the poet. Such an approach may be appropriate for Romantic and post-Romantic poetry, but it is wholly anachronistic as a way of reading a seventeenth-century poet such as Marvell, for whom poetry was an artifice designed for a reader or a listener rather than a medium to be used for an outpouring of personal feelings. 'To his Coy Mistress', for example, is not an account of a real seduction attempt: Marvell seems not to have had strong heterosexual impulses, and in a later age might have thought of himself as gay. Indeed, seduction in the seventeenth century, as now, consisted of flattery and assurances of undying affection rather than syllogistic argument, and any woman who could be seduced by such a poem would be a half-wit incapable of enjoying bathetic effects such as the juxtaposition of the Ganges and the Humber. The implied reader of the poem may be the object of the poet's erotic intentions, but the real readers of such poems were male, and the poem rests on shared male assumptions about women as consumable sexual commodities.

Marvell is a green poet, but like many of his modern counterparts, his knowledge of nature is that of the enthusiastic townsman rather than the native of the countryside. His account of the green woodpecker (which Marvell calls the hewel, its onomatopoeic name) felling trees in 'Upon Appleton House' (stanzas 68–70), for example, is ornithologically inexact, in that the green woodpecker (unlike great and lesser-spotted woodpeckers) does not drum on oaks in pursuit of wood-boring insects, but rather feeds on the ground. Marvell is not a versifying Gilbert White, but an 'easy philosopher' (stanza 71) who has used the analogy of the stricken oak to reflect on the frailty and corruption of the human body. Such reflections are characteristic of Marvell's landscape poems, which are chiefly concerned with contemplative retirement from active life. In the case of 'The Garden' the retirement is a withdrawal from fame, from crowds and from heterosexual pursuits, and Marvell adopts a relentlessly playful tone as he wittily exalts the sensuality of nature and deprecates the companionship of women with a robust misogyny destined to irritate late twentieth-century readers who do not share his attitudes. Marvell's 'Upon Appleton House', the central country-house poem of the mid seventeenth century, is an account of the Yorkshire estate to which General Fairfax retired at the age of thirty-eight after his resignation as commander-in-chief in the wake of the execution of Charles I and the proposed invasion of Scotland (Fairfax was willing to defend England, but not to initiate a war against Scotland). The surface of the poem is resolutely non-political, but, here as in Shakespeare's *Richard II*, gardening is a metaphor of good government, and so the order of the estate reflects the virtue of its master. The countryside is transformed in Marvell's poem into a picture, and its inhabitants are fleas in 'a landskip drawn in looking-glass' (stanza 58); similarly, the mown field is a plain that 'lies quilted o'er with bodies slain' – a powerful evocation of the battles of the civil war.

Marvell was for some reason quite secretive about his poetry. One consequence of his unwillingness to be known as a poet is the absence of an authoritative text of his poetry. There are no surviving manuscripts of the poems in his hand, and he never prepared an edition for publication. After he died, his landlady, Mary Palmer, assembled his poems and arranged for them to be published, signing the preface 'Mary Marvell', presumably in the hope that if she could pass herself off as Marvell's widow she might be able to claim part of his estate. In 1944 the Bodleian Library in Oxford acquired a copy of the 1681 edition that had been marked up, apparently for use as a copy-text for a second edition. This volume contains hand-written corrections to the printed poems and texts (in the same hand) of Marvell's poems on Cromwell, which had been cancelled from the 1681 edition. One of the corrections in this copy concerns the phrase 'iron gates of life' in 'To his Coy Mistress'. Tennyson had told Palgrave that ' "grates" would have intensified Marvell's image'; the discovery of the Oxford copy vindicated Tennyson's unease, because 'gates' is corrected to 'grates'. Many of the corrections in this annotated copy ring true, and I have adopted most of them in this edition.

GORDON CAMPBELL

Andrew Marvell

A Dialogue between the Resolved Soul and Created Pleasure

Courage, my Soul, now learn to wield
The weight of thine immortal shield.
Close on thy head thy helmet bright.
Balance thy sword against the fight.
See where an army, strong as fair,
With silken banners spreads the air.
Now, if thou be'st that thing divine,
In this day's combat let it shine:
And show that Nature wants an art
To conquer one resolvèd heart.   10

PLEASURE
Welcome the creation's guest,
Lord of earth, and heaven's heir.
Lay aside that warlike crest,
And of Nature's banquet share:
Where the souls of fruits and flowers
Stand prepared to heighten yours.

SOUL
I sup above, and cannot stay
To bait so long upon the way.

PLEASURE
On these downy pillows lie,
Whose soft plumes will thither fly: 20
On these roses strewed so plain
Lest one leaf thy side should strain.

SOUL
My gentler rest is on a thought,
Conscious of doing what I ought.

PLEASURE

If thou be'st with perfumes pleased,
Such as oft the gods appeased,
Thou in fragrant clouds shalt show
Like another god below.

SOUL

A soul that knows not to presume
Is heaven's and its own perfume.   30

PLEASURE

Everything does seem to vie
Which should first attract thine eye:
But since none deserves that grace,
In this crystal view thy face.

SOUL

When the Creator's skill is prized,
The rest is all but earth disguised.

PLEASURE

Hark how music then prepares
For thy stay these charming airs;
Which the posting winds recall,
And suspend the river's fall.   40

SOUL

Had I but any time to lose,
On this I would it all dispose.
Cease, tempter. None can chain a mind
Whom this sweet chordage cannot bind.

CHORUS

Earth cannot show so brave a sight
As when a single soul does fence
The batteries of alluring sense,
And heaven views it with delight.
    Then persevere: for still new charges sound:
    And if thou overcom'st, thou shalt be crowned.   50

PLEASURE

All this fair, and soft, and sweet,
   Which scatteringly doth shine,
Shall within one beauty meet,
   And she be only thine.

SOUL

If things of sight such heavens be,
What heavens are those we cannot see?

PLEASURE

Wheresoe'er thy foot shall go
   The minted gold shall lie,
Till thou purchase all below,
   And want new worlds to buy.   60

SOUL

Were't not a price, who'd value gold?
And that's worth naught that can be sold.

PLEASURE

Wilt thou all the glory have
   That war or peace commend?
Half the world shall be thy slave
   The other half thy friend.

SOUL

What friends, if to myself untrue?
What slaves, unless I captive you?

PLEASURE

Thou shalt know each hidden cause;
   And see the future time:
Try what depth the centre draws;   70
   And then to heaven climb.

SOUL
None thither mounts by the degree
Of knowledge, but humility.

CHORUS
Triumph, triumph, victorious Soul;
The world has not one pleasure more:
The rest does lie beyond the Pole,
And is thine everlasting store.

On a Drop of Dew

See how the orient dew,
Shed from the bosom of the morn
    Into the blowing roses,
Yet careless of its mansion new,
For the clear region where 'twas born
    Round in itself encloses:
    And in its little globe's extent,
Frames as it can its native element.
    How it the purple flower does slight,
        Scarce touching where it lies,   10
    But gazing back upon the skies,
        Shines with a mournful light,
            Like its own tear,
Because so long divided from the sphere.
    Restless it rolls and unsecure,
        Trembling lest it grow impure,
    Till the warm sun pity its pain,
And to the skies exhale it back again.
        So the soul, that drop, that ray
Of the clear fountain of eternal day,   20
Could it within the human flower be seen,
    Remembering still its former height,
    Shuns the swart leaves and blossoms green,
    And recollecting its own light,

Does, in its pure and circling thoughts, express
The greater heaven in an heaven less.
   In how coy a figure wound,
   Every way it turns away:
   So the world excluding round,
   Yet receiving in the day,   30
   Dark beneath, but bright above,
   Here disdaining, there in love.
How loose and easy hence to go,
How girt and ready to ascend,
Moving but on a point below,
It all about does upwards bend.
Such did the manna's sacred dew distil,
White and entire, though congealed and chill,
Congealed on earth: but does, dissolving, run
Into the glories of th' almighty sun.   40

The Coronet

When for the thorns with which I long, too long,
   With many a piercing wound,
   My saviour's head have crowned,
I seek with garlands to redress that wrong;
   Through every garden, every mead,
I gather flowers (my fruits are only flowers),
   Dismantling all the fragrant towers
That once adorned my shepherdess's head.
And now when I have summed up all my store,
   Thinking (so I myself deceive)   10
   So rich a chaplet thence to weave
As never yet the king of glory wore:
   Alas, I find the serpent old
   That, twining in his speckled breast,
   About the flowers disguised does fold,
   With wreaths of fame and interest.
Ah, foolish man, that wouldst debase with them,

And mortal glory, heaven's diadem!
But thou who only couldst the serpent tame,
Either his slippery knots at once untie,   20
And disentangle all his winding snare;
Or shatter too with him my curious frame,
And let these wither, so that he may die,
Though set with skill and chosen out with care:
That they, while thou on both their spoils dost tread,
May crown thy feet, that could not crown thy head.

Eyes and Tears

1

How wisely Nature did decree,
With the same eyes to weep and see!
That, having viewed the object vain,
We might be ready to complain.

2

Thus since the self-deluding sight,
In a false angle takes each height,
These tears, which better measure all,
Like watery lines and plummets fall.

3

Two tears, which Sorrow long did weigh
Within the scales of either eye,   10
And then paid out in equal poise,
Are the true price of all my joys.

4

What in the world most fair appears,
Yea, even laughter, turns to tears:
And all the jewels which we prize,
Melt in these pendants of the eyes.

5

I have through every garden been,
Amongst the red, the white, the green,
And yet, from all the flowers I saw,
No honey but these tears, could draw.   20

6

So the all-seeing sun each day
Distils the world with chemic ray,
But finds the essence only showers,
Which straight in pity back he pours.

7

Yet happy they whom grief doth bless,
That weep the more, and see the less:
And, to preserve their sight more true,
Bathe still their eyes in their own dew.

8

So Magdalen, in tears more wise
Dissolved those captivating eyes,   30
Whose liquid chains could flowing meet
To fetter her Redeemer's feet.

9

Not full sails hasting loaden home,
Nor the chaste lady's pregnant womb,
Nor Cynthia teeming shows so fair,
As two eyes swoll'n with weeping are.

10

The sparkling glance that shoots desire,
Drenched in these waves does lose its fire.
Yea, oft the Thunderer pity takes
And here the hissing lightning slakes.   40

11

The incense was to heaven dear,
Not as a perfume, but a tear.

And stars show lovely in the night,
But as they seem the tears of light.

12
Ope then, mine eyes, your double sluice,
And practise so your noblest use;
For others too can see, or sleep,
But only human eyes can weep.

13
Now, like two clouds dissolving, drop,
And at each tear in distance stop: 50
Now, like two fountains, trickle down;
Now, like two floods o'erturn and drown.

14
Thus let your streams o'erflow your springs,
Till eyes and tears be the same things:
And each the other's difference bears;
These weeping eyes, those seeing tears.

Bermudas

Where the remote Bermudas ride
In th' ocean's bosom unespied,
From a small boat, that rowed along,
The listening winds received this song.
  'What should we do but sing his praise
That led us through the watery maze,
Unto an isle so long unknown,
And yet far kinder than our own?
Where he the huge sea-monsters wracks,
That lift the deep upon their backs,   10
He lands us on a grassy stage,
Safe from the storms, and prelate's rage.
He gave us this eternal spring,
Which here enamels everything,

And sends the fowl to us in care,
On daily visits through the air.
He hangs in shades the orange bright,
Like golden lamps in a green night,
And does in the pom'granates close
Jewels more rich than Ormus shows.   20
He makes the figs our mouths to meet,
And throws the melons at our feet,
But apples plants of such a price,
No tree could ever bear them twice.
With cedars, chosen by his hand,
From Lebanon, he stores the land,
And makes the hollow seas, that roar,
Proclaim the ambergris on shore.
He cast (of which we rather boast)
The gospel's pearl upon our coast,   30
And in these rocks for us did frame
A temple, where to sound his name.
Oh let our voice his praise exalt,
Till it arrive at heaven's vault:
Which thence (perhaps) rebounding, may
Echo beyond the Mexique Bay.'
    Thus sung they, in the English boat,
An holy and a cheerful note,
And all the way, to guide their chime,
With falling oars they kept the time.

Clorinda and Damon

CLORINDA   Damon, come drive thy flocks this way.
  DAMON   No, 'tis too late; they went astray.
CLORINDA   I have a grassy scutcheon spied,
           Where Flora blazons all her pride.
           The grass I aim to feast thy sheep:
           The flowers I for thy temples keep.
  DAMON   Grass withers; and the flowers too fade.

CLORINDA	Seize the short joys then, ere they vade,
	Seest thou that unfrequented cave?
DAMON	That den?
CLORINDA	Love's shrine.
DAMON	But virtue's grave.
CLORINDA	In whose cool bosom we may lie
	Safe from the sun.
DAMON	Not heaven's eye.
CLORINDA	Near this, a fountain's liquid bell
	Tinkles within the concave shell.
DAMON	Might a soul bathe there and be clean,
	Or slake its drought?
CLORINDA	What is't you mean?
DAMON	These once had been enticing things,
	Clorinda, pastures, caves, and springs.
CLORINDA	And what late change?
DAMON	The other day
	Pan met me.
CLORINDA	What did great Pan say?
DAMON	Words that transcend poor shepherds' skill,
	But he e'er since my songs does fill:
	And his name swells my slender oat.
CLORINDA	Sweet must Pan sound in Damon's note.
DAMON	Clorinda's voice might make it sweet.
CLORINDA	Who would not in Pan's praises meet?

The numbers 10 and 20 appear in the right margin at lines 10 and 20.

CHORUS

Of Pan the flowery pastures sing,
Caves echo, and the fountains ring.
Sing then while he doth us inspire;
For all the world is our Pan's choir.

A Dialogue between the Soul and Body

SOUL

O, who shall from this dungeon raise
A soul, enslaved so many ways,
With bolts of bones, that fettered stands
In feet, and manacled in hands
Here blinded with an eye; and there
Deaf with the drumming of an ear,
A soul hung up, as 'twere, in chains
Of nerves, and arteries, and veins,
Tortured, besides each other part,
In a vain head, and double heart? 10

BODY

O, who shall me deliver whole,
From bonds of this tyrannic soul,
Which, stretched upright, impales me so,
That mine own precipice I go;
And warms and moves this needless frame
(A fever could but do the same),
And, wanting where its spite to try,
Has made me live to let me die,
A body that could never rest,
Since this ill spirit it possessed? 20

SOUL

What magic could me thus confine
Within another's grief to pine,
Where, whatsoever it complain,
I feel, that cannot feel, the pain,
And all my care itself employs,
That to preserve, which me destroys:
Constrained not only to endure
Diseases, but, what's worse, the cure:
And ready oft the port to gain,
Am shipwrecked into health again? 30

BODY
But physic yet could never reach
The maladies thou me dost teach:
Whom first the cramp of hope does tear,
And then the palsy shakes of fear;
The pestilence of love does heat,
Or hatred's hidden ulcer eat;
Joy's cheerful madness does perplex,
Or sorrow's other madness vex;
Which knowledge forces me to know,
And memory will not forgo.   40
What but a soul could have the wit
To build me up for sin so fit?
So architects do square and hew,
Green trees that in the forest grew.

The Nymph Complaining for the Death of her Fawn

The wanton troopers riding by
Have shot my fawn, and it will die.
Ungentle men! They cannot thrive
To kill thee! Thou ne'er didst alive
Them any harm: alas, nor could
Thy death yet do them any good.
I'm sure I never wished them ill;
Nor do I for all this; nor will:
But if my simple prayers may yet
Prevail with heaven to forget   10
Thy murder, I will join my tears
Rather than fail. But, O my fears!
It cannot die so. Heaven's King
Keeps register of everything:
And nothing may we use in vain.
E'en beasts must be with justice slain,

Else men are made their deodands.
Though they should wash their guilty hands
In this warm life-blood, which doth part
From thine, and wound me to the heart,   20
Yet could they not be clean: their stain
Is dyed in such a purple grain,
There is not such another in
The world, to offer for their sin.
  Unconstant Sylvio, when yet
I had not found him counterfeit,
One morning (I remember well),
Tied in this silver chain and bell
Gave it to me: nay, and I know
What he said then; I'm sure I do.   30
Said he, 'Look how your huntsman here
Hath taught a fawn to hunt his dear.'
But Sylvio soon had me beguiled.
This waxèd tame, while he grew wild,
And quite regardless of my smart,
Left me his fawn, but took his heart.
  Thenceforth I set myself to play
My solitary time away
With this: and very well content,
Could so mine idle life have spent.   40
For it was full of sport; and light
Of foot, and heart; and did invite
Me to its game; it seemed to bless
Itself in me. How could I less
Than love it? O I cannot be
Unkind, t'a beast that loveth me.
  Had it lived long, I do not know
Whether it too might have done so
As Sylvio did: his gifts might be
Perhaps as false or more than he.   50
But I am sure, for ought that I
Could in so short a time espy,
Thy love was far more better than
The love of false and cruel men.
  With sweetest milk, and sugar, first
I it at mine own fingers nursed.

And as it grew, so every day
It waxed more white and sweet than they.
It had so sweet a breath! And oft
I blushed to see its foot more soft,   60
And white (shall I say than my hand?)
Nay, any lady's of the land.
    It is a wondrous thing, how fleet
'Twas on those little silver feet.
With what a pretty skipping grace,
It oft would challenge me the race:
And when 't had left me far away,
'Twould stay, and run again, and stay.
For it was nimbler much than hinds;
And trod, as on the foúr winds.   70
    I have a garden of my own
But so with roses overgrown,
And lilies, that you would it guess
To be a little wilderness.
And all the springtime of the year
It only lovèd to be there.
Among the beds of lilies, I
Have sought it oft, where it should lie;
Yet could not, till itself would rise,
Find it, although before mine eyes.   80
For, in the flaxen lilies' shade,
It like a bank of lilies laid.
Upon the roses it would feed,
Until its lips e'en seemed to bleed:
And then to me 'twould boldly trip,
And print those roses on my lip.
But all its chief delight was still
On roses thus itself to fill:
And its pure virgin limbs to fold
In whitest sheets of lilies cold.   90
Had it lived long, it would have been
Lilies without, roses within.
    O help! O help! I see it faint:
And die as calmly as a saint.
See how it weeps. The tears do come
Sad, slowly dropping like a gum.

So weeps the wounded balsam: so
The holy frankincense doth flow.
The brotherless Heliades
Melt in such amber tears as these.   100
   I in a golden vial will
Keep these two crystal tears; and fill
It till it do o'erflow with mine;
Then place it in Diana's shrine.
   Now my sweet fawn is vanished to
Whither the swans and turtles go:
In fair Elysium to endure,
With milk-white lambs, and ermines pure.
O do not run too fast: for I
Will but bespeak thy grave, and die.   110
   First my unhappy statue shall
Be cut in marble; and withal,
Let it be weeping too ; but there
The engraver sure his art may spare,
For I so truly thee bemoan,
That I shall weep though I be stone:
Until my tears (still dropping) wear
My breast, themselves engraving there.
Then at my feet shalt thou be laid,
Of purest alabaster made: 120
For I would have thine image be
White as I can, though not as thee.

Young Love

1

Come, little infant, love me now,
   While thine unsuspected years
Clear thine aged father's brow
   From cold jealousy and fears.

2

Pretty, surely, 'twere to see
   By young love old time beguiled,
While our sportings are as free
   As the nurse's with the child.

3

Common beauties stay fifteen;
   Such as yours should swifter move,   10
Whose fair blossoms are too green
   Yet for lust, but not for love.

4

Love as much the snowy lamb,
   Or the wanton kid, does prize,
As the lusty bull or ram,
   For his morning sacrifice.

5

Now then love me: time may take
   Thee before thy time away:
Of this need we'll virtue make,
   And learn love before we may.   20

6

So we win of doubtful fate;
   And, if good she to us meant,
We that good shall antedate,
   Or, if ill, that ill prevent.

7

Thus as kingdoms, frustrating
   Other titles to their crown,
In the cradle crown their king,
   So all foreign claims to drown,

8

So, to make all rivals vain,
   Now I crown thee with my love: 30
Crown me with thy love again,
   And we both shall monarchs prove.

To his Coy Mistress

Had we but world enough, and time,
This coyness, Lady, were no crime.
We would sit down, and think which way
To walk, and pass our long love's day.
Thou by the Indian Ganges' side
Should'st rubies find: I by the tide
Of Humber would complain. I would
Love you ten years before the flood:
And you should, if you please, refuse
Till the conversion of the Jews.   10
My vegetable love should grow
Vaster than empires, and more slow.
An hundred years should go to praise
Thine eyes, and on thy forehead gaze.
Two hundred to adore each breast:
But thirty thousand to the rest.
An age at least to every part,
And the last age should show your heart:
For, Lady, you deserve this state;
Nor would I love at lower rate.   20
    But at my back I always hear
Time's wingèd chariot hurrying near:
And yonder all before us lie
Deserts of vast eternity.
Thy beauty shall no more be found;
Nor, in thy marble vault, shall sound
My echoing song: then worms shall try
That long-preserved virginity:
And your quaint honour turn to dust;
And into ashes all my lust.   30
The grave's a fine and private place,
But none, I think, do there embrace.
    Now, therefore, while the youthful hue
Sits on thy skin like morning dew,
And while thy willing soul transpires
At every pore with instant fires,
Now let us sport us while we may;

And now, like amorous birds of prey,
Rather at once our time devour,
Than languish in his slow-chapped power.   40
Let us roll our strength, and all
Our sweetness, up into one ball:
And tear our pleasures with rough strife,
Thorough the iron grates of life.
Thus, though we cannot make our sun
Stand still, yet we will make him run.

The Unfortunate Lover

1

Alas, how pleasant are their days
With whom the infant Love yet plays!
Sorted by pairs, they still are seen
By fountains cool, and shadows green.
But soon these flames do lose their light,
Like meteors of a summer's night:
Nor can they to that region climb,
To make impression upon time.

2

'Twas in a shipwreck, when the seas
Ruled, and the winds did what they please,   10
That my poor lover floating lay,
And, ere brought forth, was cast away:
Till at the last the master-wave
Upon the rock his mother drave;
And there she split against the stone,
In a Caesarean sectión.

3

The sea him lent those bitter tears
Which at his eyes he always wears;
And from the winds the sighs he bore,

Which through his surging breast do roar.   20
No day he saw but that which breaks
Through frighted crowds in forkèd streaks,
While round the rattling thunder hurled,
As at the funeral of the world.

4

While Nature to his birth presents
This masque of quarrelling elements,
A numerous fleet of cormorants black,
That sailed insulting o'er the wrack,
Received into their cruel care
Th' unfortunate and abject heir: 30
Guardians most fit to entertain
The orphan of the hurricane.

5

They fed him up with hopes and air,
Which soon digested to despair,
And as one cormorant fed him, still
Another on his heart did bill,
Thus while they famish him, and feast,
He both consumèd, and increased:
And languishèd with doubtful breath,
The amphibium of life and death.   40

6

And now, when angry heaven would
Behold a spectacle of blood,
Fortune and he are called to play
At sharp before it all the day:
And tyrant Love his breast does ply
With all his winged artillery,
Whilst he, betwixt the flames and waves,
Like Ajax, the mad tempest braves.

7

See how he nak'd and fierce does stand,
Cuffing the thunder with one hand,   50
While with the other he does lock,

And grapple, with the stubborn rock:
From which he with each wave rebounds,
Torn into flames, and ragg'd with wounds,
And all he 'says, a lover dressed
In his own blood does relish best.

8

This is the only banneret
That ever Love created yet:
Who though, by the malignant stars,
Forcèd to live in storms and wars,   60
Yet dying leaves a perfume here,
And music within every ear:
And he in story only rules,
In a field sable a lover gules.

The Gallery

1

Clora, come view my soul, and tell
Whether I have contrived it well.
Now all its several lodgings lie
Composed into one gallery;
And the great arras-hangings, made
Of various faces, by are laid;
That, for all furniture, you'll find
Only your picture in my mind.

2

Here thou are painted in the dress
Of an inhuman murderess;   10
Examining upon our hearts
Thy fertile shop of cruel arts:
Engines more keen than ever yet
Adornèd tyrant's cabinet;

Of which the most tormenting are
Black eyes, red lips, and curlèd hair.

3

But, on the other side, th'art drawn
Like to Aurora in the dawn;
When in the East she slumbering lies,
And stretches out her milky thighs;   20
While all the morning choir does sing,
And manna falls, and roses spring;
And, at thy feet, the wooing doves
Sit pérfecting their harmless loves.

4

Like an enchantress here thou show'st,
Vexing thy restless lover's ghost;
And, by a light obscure, dost rave
Over his entrails, in the cave;
Divining thence, with horrid care,
How long thou shalt continue fair;   30
And (when informed) them throw'st away,
To be the greedy vulture's prey.

5

But, against that, thou sit'st afloat
Like Venus in her pearly boat.
The halcyons, calming all that's nigh,
Betwixt the air and water fly;
Or, if some rolling wave appears,
A mass of ambergris it bears.
Nor blows more wind than what may well
Convoy the perfume to the smell.   40

6

These pictures and a thousand more
Of thee my gallery do store
In all the forms thou canst invent
Either to please me, or torment:

For thou alone to people me,
Art grown a numerous colony;
And a collection choicer far
Than or Whitehall's or Mantua's were.

                    7
But, of these pictures and the rest,
That at the entrance likes me best: 50
Where the same posture, and the look
Remains, with which I first was took:
A tender shepherdess, whose hair
Hangs loosely playing in the air,
Transplanting flowers from the green hill,
To crown her head, and bosom fill.

The Fair Singer

                    1
To make a final conquest of all me,
Love did compose so sweet an enemy,
In whom both beauties to my death agree,
Joining themselves in fatal harmony;
That while she with her eyes my heart does bind,
She with her voice might captivate my mind.

                    2
I could have fled from one but singly fair:
My disentangled soul itself might save,
Breaking the curlèd trammels of her hair;
But how should I avoid to be her slave,   10
Whose subtle art invisibly can wreathe
My fetters of the very air I breathe?

                    3
It had been easy fighting in some plain,
Where victory might hang in equal choice.

But all resistance against her is vain,
Who has th' advantage both of eyes and voice,
And all my forces needs must be undone,
She having gainèd both the wind and sun.

Mourning

1

You, that decipher out the fate
Of human offsprings from the skies,
What mean these infants which of late
Spring from the stars of Clora's eyes?

2

Her eyes confused, and doubled o'er,
With tears suspended ere they flow,
Seem bending upwards, to restore
To heaven, whence it came, their woe.

3

When, moulding of the watery spheres,
Slow drops untie themselves away,   10
As if she, with those precious tears,
Would strow the ground where Strephon lay.

4

Yet some affirm, pretending art,
Her eyes have so her bosom drowned,
Only to soften near her heart
A place to fix another wound.

5

And, while vain pomp does her restrain
Within her solitary bow'r,
She courts herself in am'rous rain;
Herself both Danaë and the show'r.   20

6

Nay, others, bolder, hence esteem
Joy now so much her master grown,
That whatsoever does but seem
Like grief, is from her windows thrown.

7

Nor that she pays, while she survives,
To her dead love this tribute due,
But casts abroad these donatives,
At the installing of a new.

8

How wide they dream! The Indian slaves
That dive for pearl through seas profound   30
Would find her tears yet deeper waves
And not of one the bottom sound.

9

I yet my silent judgement keep,
Disputing not what they believe:
But sure as oft as women weep,
It is to be supposed they grieve.

Daphnis and Chloe

1

Daphnis must from Chloe part:
Now is come the dismal hour
That must all his hopes devour,
All his labour, all his art.

2

Nature, her own sex's foe,
Long had taught her to be coy:

But she neither knew t'enjoy,
Nor yet let her lover go.

3

But with this sad news surprised,
Soon she let that niceness fall,   10
And would gladly yield to all,
So it had his stay comprised.

4

Nature so herself does use
To lay by her wonted state,
Lest the world should separate;
Sudden parting closer glues.

5

He, well-read in all the ways
By which men their siege maintain,
Knew not that the fort to gain,
Better 'twas the siege to raise.   20

6

But he came so full possessed
With the grief of parting thence,
That he had not so much sense
As to see he might be blessed.

7

Till Love in her language breathed
Words she never spake before,
But than legacies no more
To a dying man bequeathed.

8

For, alas, the time was spent,
Now the latest minute's run   30
When poor Daphnis is undone,
Between joy and sorrow rent.

9

At that 'Why', that 'Stay, my dear',
His disordered locks he tare;
And with rolling eyes did glare,
And his cruel fate forswear.

10

As the soul of one scarce dead,
With the shrieks of friends aghast,
Looks distracted back in haste,
And then straight again is fled,   40

11

So did wretched Daphnis look,
Frighting her he lovèd most.
At the last, this lover's ghost
Thus his leave resolvèd took.

12

'Are my hell and heaven joined
More to torture him that dies?
Could departure not suffice,
But that you must then grow kind?

13

'Ah, my Chloe, how have I
Such a wretched minute found,   50
When thy favours should me wound
More than all thy cruelty?

14

'So to the condemnèd wight
The delicious cup we fill;
And allow him all he will,
For his last and short delight.

15

'But I will not now begin
Such a debt unto my foe;

Nor to my departure owe
What my presence could not win.   60

16

'Absence is too much alone:
Better 'tis to go in peace,
Than my losses to increase
By a late fruition.

17

'Why should I enrich my fate?
'Tis a vanity to wear,
For my executioner,
Jewels of so high a rate.

18

'Rather I away will pine
In a manly stubbornness
Than be fatted up express   70
For the cannibal to dine.

19

'Whilst this grief does thee disarm,
All th' enjoyment of our love
But the ravishment would prove
Of a body dead while warm.

20

'And I parting should appear
Like the gourmand Hebrew dead,
While with quails and manna fed,
He does through the desert err.   80

21

'Or the witch that midnight wakes
For the fern, whose magic weed
In one minute casts the seed,
And invisible him makes.

22

'Gentler times for love are meant:
Who for parting pleasure strain
Gather roses in the rain,
Wet themselves and spoil their scent.

23

'Farewell, therefore, all the fruit
Which I could from love receive: 90
Joy will not with sorrow weave,
Nor will I this grief pollute.

24

'Fate, I come, as dark, as sad,
As thy malice could desire;
Yet bring with me all the fire
That Love in his torches had.'

25

At these words away he broke;
As who long has praying li'n,
To his headsman makes the sign,
And receives the parting stroke.   100

26

But hence, virgins, all beware:
Last night he with Phlogis slept;
This night for Dorinda kept;
And but rid to take the air.

27

Yet he does himself excuse;
Nor indeed without a cause:
For, according to the laws,
Why did Chloe once refuse?

The Definition of Love

1

My love is of a birth as rare
As 'tis for object strange and high:
It was begotten by Despair
Upon Impossibility.

2

Magnanimous Despair alone
Could show me so divine a thing,
Where feeble Hope could ne'er have flown
But vainly flapped its tinsel wing.

3

And yet I quickly might arrive
Where my extended soul is fixed,   10
But Fate does iron wedges drive,
And always crowds itself betwixt.

4

For Fate with jealous eye does see
Two perfect loves, nor lets them close:
Their union would her ruin be,
And her tyrannic power depose.

5

And therefore her decrees of steel
Us as the distant poles have placed,
(Though Love's whole world on us doth wheel)
Not by themselves to be embraced,   20

6

Unless the giddy heaven fall,
And earth some new convulsion tear;
And, us to join, the world should all
Be cramped into a planisphere.

7

As lines (so loves) oblique may well
Themselves in every angle greet:
But ours so truly parallel,
Though infinite, can never meet.

8

Therefore the love which us doth bind,
But Fate so enviously debars,   30
Is the conjunction of the mind,
And opposition of the stars.

The Picture of Little T.C.
in a Prospect of Flowers

1

See with what simplicity
This nymph begins her golden days!
In the green grass she loves to lie,
And there with her fair aspect tames
The wilder flowers, and gives them names:
But only with the roses plays;
                And them does tell
What colour best becomes them, and what smell.

2

Who can foretell for what high cause
This darling of the gods was born!   10
Yet this is she whose chaster laws
The wanton Love shall one day fear,
And, under her command severe,
See his bow broke and ensigns torn.
                Happy, who can
Appease this virtuous enemy of man!

3

O, then let me in time compound,
And parley with those conquering eyes;
Ere they have tried their force to wound,
Ere, with their glancing wheels, they drive   20
In triumph over hearts that strive,
And them that yield but more despise.
              Let me be laid,
Where I may see thy glories from some shade.

4

Meantime, whilst every verdant thing
Itself does at thy beauty charm,
Reform the errors of the spring;
Make that the tulips may have share
Of sweetness, seeing they are fair;
And roses of their thorns disarm: 30
              But most procure
That violets may a longer age endure.

5

But, O young beauty of the woods,
Whom Nature courts with fruits and flowers,
Gather the flowers, but spare the buds;
Lest Flora angry at thy crime,
To kill her infants in their prime,
Do quickly make th' example yours;
              And, ere we see,
Nip in the blossom all our hopes and thee.

The Match

1

Nature had long a treasure made
   Of all her choicest store;
Fearing, when she should be decayed,
   To beg in vain for more.

2

Her orientest colours there,
    And essences most pure,
With sweetest perfumes hoarded were,
    All, as she thought, secure.

3

She seldom them unlocked, or used,
    But with the nicest care;
For, with one grain of them diffused,
    She could the world repair.

10

4

But likeness soon together drew
    What she did sep'rate lay;
Of which one perfect beauty grew,
    And that was Celia.

5

Love wisely had of long foreseen
    That he must once grow old;
And therefore stored a magazine,
    To save him from the cold.

20

6

He kept the several cells replete
    With nitre thrice refined;
The naphtha's and the sulphur's heat,
    And all that burns the mind.

7

He fortified the double gate,
    And rarely thither came;
For, with one spark of these, he straight
    All Nature could inflame.

8

Till, by vicinity so long,
    A nearer way they sought;   30
And, grown magnetically strong,
    Into each other wrought.

9

Thus all his fuel did unite
    To make one fire high:
None ever burned so hot, so bright:
    And, Celia, that am I.

10

So we alone the happy rest,
    Whilst all the world is poor,
And have within ourselves possessed
    All Love's and Nature's store.   40

The Mower against Gardens

Luxurious man, to bring his vice in use,
    Did after him the world seduce,
And from the fields the flowers and plants allure,
    Where nature was most plain and pure.
He first enclosed within the gardens square
    A dead and standing pool of air,
And a more luscious earth for them did knead,
    Which stupified them while it fed.
The pink grew then as double as his mind;
    The nutriment did change the kind.   10
With strange perfumes he did the roses taint,
    And flowers themselves were taught to paint.
The tulip, white, did for complexion seek,
    And learned to interline its cheek:
Its onion root they then so high did hold,
    That one was for a meadow sold.

Another world was searched, through oceans new,
　　To find the Marvel of Peru.
And yet these rarities might be allowed
　　To man, that sovereign thing and proud,   20
Had he not dealt between the bark and tree,
　　Forbidden mixtures there to see.
No plant now knew the stock from which it came;
　　He grafts upon the wild the tame:
That th' uncertain and adulterate fruit
　　Might put the palate in dispute.
His green seraglio has its eunuchs too,
　　Lest any tyrant him outdo.
And in the cherry he does nature vex,
　　To procreate without a sex.   30
'Tis all enforced, the fountain and the grot,
　　While the sweet fields do lie forgot:
Where willing nature does to all dispense
　　A wild and fragrant innocence:
And fauns and fairies do the meadows till,
　　More by their presence than their skill.
Their statues, polished by some ancient hand,
　　May to adorn the gardens stand:
But howsoe'er the figures do excel,
　　The gods themselves with us do dwell.

Damon the Mower

1

Hark how the Mower Damon sung,
With love of Juliana stung!
While everything did seem to paint
The scene more fit for his complaint.
Like her fair eyes the day was fair,
But scorching like his am'rous care.
Sharp like his scythe his sorrow was,
And withered like his hopes the grass.

2

'Oh what unusual heats are here,
Which thus our sunburned meadows sear!   10
The grasshopper its pipe gives o'er;
And hamstringed frogs can dance no more.
But in the brook the green frog wades;
And grasshoppers seek out the shades.
Only the snake, that kept within,
Now glitters in its second skin.

3

'This heat the sun could never raise,
Nor Dog Star so inflame the days.
It from an higher beauty grow'th,
Which burns the fields and mower both: 20
Which mads the dog, and makes the sun
Hotter than his own Phaëton.
Not July causeth these extremes,
But Juliana's scorching beams.

4

'Tell me where I may pass the fires
Of the hot day, or hot desires.
To what cool cave shall I descend,
Or to what gelid fountain bend?
Alas! I look for ease in vain,
When remedies themselves complain.   30
No moisture but my tears do rest,
Nor cold but in her icy breast.

5

'How long wilt thou, fair shepherdess,
Esteem me, and my presents less?
To thee the harmless snake I bring,
Disarmèd of its teeth and sting;
To thee chameleons, changing hue,
And oak leaves tipped with honey dew.
Yet thou, ungrateful, hast not sought
Nor what they are, nor who them brought.   40

6

'I am the Mower Damon, known
Through all the meadows I have mown.
On me the morn her dew distils
Before her darling daffodils.
And, if at noon my toil me heat,
The sun himself licks off my sweat.
While, going home, the evening sweet
In cowslip-water bathes my feet.

7

'What, though the piping shepherd stock
The plains with an unnumbered flock,   50
This scythe of mine discovers wide
More ground than all his sheep do hide.
With this the golden fleece I shear
Of all these closes every year.
And though in wool more poor than they,
Yet am I richer far in hay.

8

'Nor am I so deformed to sight,
If in my scythe I lookèd right;
In which I see my picture done,
As in a crescent moon the sun.   60
The deathless fairies take me oft
To lead them in their dances soft:
And, when I tune myself to sing,
About me they contract their ring.

9

'How happy might I still have mowed,
Had not Love here his thistles sowed!
But now I all the day complain,
Joining my labour to my pain;
And with my scythe cut down the grass,
Yet still my grief is where it was: 70
But, when the iron blunter grows,
Sighing, I whet my scythe and woes.'

10

While thus he threw his elbow round,
Depopulating all the ground,
And, with his whistling scythe, does cut
Each stroke between the earth and root,
The edgèd steel by careless chance
Did into his own ankle glance;
And there among the grass fell down,
By his own scythe, the Mower mown.   80

11

'Alas!' said he, 'these hurts are slight
To those that die by love's despite.
With shepherd's-purse, and clown's-all-heal,
The blood I staunch, and wound I seal.
Only for him no cure is found,
Whom Juliana's eyes do wound.
'Tis death alone that this must do:
For Death thou art a Mower too.'

The Mower to the Glow-worms

1

Ye living lamps, by whose dear light
The nightingale does sit so late,
And studying all the summer night,
Her matchless songs does meditate;

2

Ye country comets, that portend
No war, nor prince's funeral,
Shining unto no higher end
Than to presage the grass's fall;

3

Ye glowworms, whose officious flame
To wandering mowers shows the way,   10
That in the night have lost their aim,
And after foolish fires do stray;

4

Your courteous lights in vain you waste,
Since Juliana here is come,
For she my mind hath so displaced
That I shall never find my home.

The Mower's Song

1

My mind was once the true survey
Of all these meadows fresh and gay,
And in the greenness of the grass
Did see its hopes as in a glass;
When Juliana came, and she
What I do to the grass, does to my thoughts and me.

2

But these, while I with sorrow pine,
Grew more luxuriant still and fine,
That not one blade of grass you spied,
But had a flower on either side;   10
When Juliana came, and she
What I do to the grass, does to my thoughts and me.

3

Unthankful meadows, could you so
A fellowship so true forgo,
And in your gaudy May-games meet,
While I lay trodden under feet?

When Juliana came, and she
What I do to the grass, does to my thoughts and me.

4

But what you in compassion ought,
Shall now by my revenge be wrought: 20
And flow'rs, and grass, and I and all,
Will in one common ruin fall.
For Juliana comes, and she
What I do to the grass, does to my thoughts and me.

5

And thus, ye meadows, which have been
Companions of my thoughts more green,
Shall now the heraldry become
With which I will adorn my tomb;
For Juliana comes, and she
What I do to the grass, does to my thoughts and me.   30

Ametas and Thestylis Making Hay-ropes

1

AMETAS
Think'st thou that this love can stand,
Whilst thou still dost say me nay?
Love unpaid does soon disband:
Love binds love as hay binds hay.

2

THESTYLIS
Think'st thou that this rope would twine
If we both should turn one way?
Where both parties so combine,
Neither love will twist nor hay.

3

AMETAS
Thus you vain excuses find,
Which yourselves and us delay: 10
And love ties a woman's mind
Looser than with ropes of hay.

4

THESTYLIS
What you cannot constant hope
Must be taken as you may.

5

AMETAS
Then let's both lay by our rope,
And go kiss within the hay.

Music's Empire

1

First was the world as one great cymbal made,
Where jarring winds to infant Nature played.
All music was a solitary sound,
To hollow rocks and murmuring fountains bound.

2

Jubal first made the wilder notes agree;
And Jubal tuned music's first jubilee:
He called the echoes from their sullen cell,
And built the organ's city where they dwell.

3

Each sought a consort in that lovely place;
And virgin trebles wed the manly bass.   10
From whence the progeny of numbers new
Into harmonious colonies withdrew.

4

Some to the lute, some to the viol went,
And others chose the cornet eloquent,
These practising the wind, and those the wire,
To sing men's triumphs, or in heaven's choir.

5

Then music, the mosaic of the air,
Did of all these a solemn noise prepare:
With which she gained the empire of the ear,
Including all between the earth and sphere.   20

6

Victorious sounds! Yet here your homage do
Unto a gentler conqueror than you:
Who though he flies the music of his praise,
Would with you heaven's hallelujahs raise.

The Garden

1

How vainly men themselves amaze
To win the palm, the oak, or bays,
And their uncessant labours see
Crowned from some single herb or tree,
Whose short and narrow vergèd shade
Does prudently their toils upbraid,
While all flow'rs and all trees do close
To weave the garlands of repose.

2

Fair Quiet, have I found thee here,
And Innocence, thy sister dear!   10
Mistaken long, I sought you then
In busy companies of men.

Your sacred plants, if here below,
Only among the plants will grow.
Society is all but rude,
To this delicious solitude.

3

No white nor red was ever seen
So am'rous as this lovely green.
Fond lovers, cruel as their flame,
Cut in these trees their mistress' name.   20
Little, alas, they know, or heed,
How far these beauties hers exceed!
Fair trees! wheres'e'er your barks I wound,
No name shall but your own be found.

4

When we have run our passion's heat,
Love hither makes his best retreat.
The gods, that mortal beauty chase,
Still in a tree did end their race.
Apollo hunted Daphne so,
Only that she might laurel grow.   30
And Pan did after Syrinx speed,
Not as a nymph, but for a reed.

5

What wondrous life is this I lead!
Ripe apples drop about my head;
The luscious clusters of the vine
Upon my mouth do crush their wine;
The nectarine, and curious peach,
Into my hands themselves do reach;
Stumbling on melons, as I pass,
Ensnared with flowers, I fall on grass.   40

6

Meanwhile the mind, from pleasures less,
Withdraws into its happiness:

The mind, that ocean where each kind
Does straight its own resemblance find,
Yet it creates, transcending these,
Far other worlds, and other seas,
Annihilating all that's made
To a green thought in a green shade.

7

Here at the fountain's sliding foot,
Or at some fruit-tree's mossy root,   50
Casting the body's vest aside,
My soul into the boughs does glide:
There like a bird it sits, and sings,
Then whets, and combs its silver wings;
And, till prepared for longer flight,
Waves in its plumes the various light.

8

Such was that happy garden-state,
While man there walked without a mate:
After a place so pure, and sweet,
What other help could yet be meet!   60
But 'twas beyond a mortal's share
To wander solitary there:
Two paradises 'twere in one
To live in paradise alone.

9

How well the skilful gardener drew
Of flowers and herbs this dial new,
Where from above the milder sun
Does through a fragrant zodiac run;
And, as it works, the industrious bee
Computes its time as well as we.   70
How could such sweet and wholesome hours
Be reckoned but with herbs and flowers!

An Horatian Ode upon Cromwell's Return from Ireland

The forward youth that would appear
Must now forsake his muses dear,
   Nor in the shadows sing
   His numbers languishing.
'Tis time to leave the books in dust,
And oil th' unusèd armour's rust:
   Removing from the wall
   The corslet of the hall.
So restless Cromwell could not cease
In the inglorious arts of peace,   10
   But through adventurous war
   Urgèd his active star.
And, like the three-forked lightning, first
Breaking the clouds where it was nursed,
   Did thorough his own side
   His fiery way divide.
(For 'tis all one to courage high
The emulous or enemy:
   And with such to enclose
   Is more than to oppose.)   20
Then burning through the air he went,
And palaces and temples rent:
   And Caesar's head at last
   Did through his laurels blast.
'Tis madness to resist or blame
The force of angry heaven's flame:
   And, if we would speak true,
   Much to the man is due,
Who, from his private gardens, where
He lived reservèd and austere,   30
   As if his highest plot
   To plant the bergamot,
Could by industrious valour climb
To ruin the great work of time,
   And cast the kingdoms old

Into another mould.
Though justice against fate complain,
And plead the ancient rights in vain:
    But those do hold or break
    As men are strong or weak.   40
Nature, that hateth emptiness,
Allows of penetration less:
    And therefore must make room
    Where greater spirits come
What field of all the Civil Wars,
Where his were not the deepest scars?
    And Hampton shows what part
    He had of wiser art,
Where, twining subtle fears with hope,
He wove a net of such a scope,   50
    That Charles himself might chase
    To Carisbrooke's narrow case:
That thence the royal actor born
The tragic scaffold might adorn:
    While round the armèd bands
    Did clap their bloody hands.
He nothing common did or mean
Upon that memorable scene:
    But with his keener eye
    The axe's edge did try: 60
Nor called the gods with vulgar spite
To vindicate his helpless right,
    But bowed his comely head,
    Down, as upon a bed.
This was that memorable hour
Which first assured the forcèd power.
    So when they did design
    The Capitol's first line,
A bleeding head where they begun,
Did fright the architects to run;   70
    And yet in that the state
    Foresaw its happy fate.
And now the Irish are ashamed
To see themselves in one year tamed:
    So much one man can do,

That does both act and know.
They can affirm his praises best,
And have, though overcome, confessed
    How good he is, how just,
    And fit for highest trust: 80
Nor yet grown stiffer with command,
But still in the Republic's hand:
    How fit he is to sway
    That can so well obey.
He to the Commons' feet presents
A kingdom, for his first year's rents:
    And, what he may, forbears
    His fame, to make it theirs:
And has his sword and spoils ungirt,
To lay them at the public's skirt.   90
    So when the falcon high
    Falls heavy from the sky,
She, having killed, no more does search
But on the next green bough to perch,
    Where, when he first does lure,
    The falc'ner has her sure.
What may not then our isle presume
While Victory his crest does plume?
    What may not others fear
    If thus he crowns each year?   100
A Caesar, he, ere long to Gaul,
To Italy an Hannibal,
    And to all states not free
    Shall climactéric be.
The Pict no shelter now shall find
Within his parti-coloured mind,
    But from this valour sad
    Shrink underneath the plaid:
Happy, if in the tufted brake
The English hunter him mistake,   110
    Nor lay his hounds in near
    The Caledonian deer.
But thou, the wars' and Fortune's son,
March indefatigably on,

And for the last effect
Still keep thy sword erect:
Besides the force it has to fright
The spirits of the shady night,
The same arts that did gain
A power, must it maintain.   120

Upon the Hill and Grove at Bilbrough

To the Lord Fairfax

1

See how the archèd earth does here
Rise in a perfect hemisphere!
The stiffest compass could not strike
A line more circular and like;
Nor softest pencil draw a brow
So equal as this hill does bow.
It seems as for a model laid,
And that the world by it was made.

2

Here learn, ye mountains more unjust,
Which to abrupter greatness thrust,   10
That do with your hook-shouldered height
The earth deform and heaven fright,
For whose excrescence, ill-designed,
Nature must a new centre find,
Learn here those humble steps to tread,
Which to securer glory lead.

3

See what a soft access and wide
Lies open to its grassy side;

Nor with the rugged path deters
The feet of breathless travellers.   20
See then how courteous it ascends,
And all the way it rises bends;
Nor for itself the height does gain,
But only strives to raise the plain.

4

Yet thus it all the field commands,
And in unenvied greatness stands,
Discerning further than the cliff
Of heaven-daring Tenerife.
How glad the weary seamen haste
When they salute it from the mast!   30
By night the Northern Star their way
Directs, and this no less by day.

5

Upon its crest this mountain grave
A plump of agèd trees does wave.
No hostile hand durst ere invade
With impious steel the sacred shade.
For something always did appear
Of the great master's terror there:
And men could hear his armour still
Rattling through all the grove and hill.   40

6

Fear of the master, and respect
Of the great nymph, did it protect,
Vera the nymph that him inspired,
To whom he often here retired,
And on these oaks engraved her name;
Such wounds alone these woods became:
But ere he well the barks could part
'Twas writ already in their heart.

7

For they ('tis credible) have sense,
As we, of love and reverence,   50
And underneath the coarser rind
The genius of the house do bind.
Hence they successes seem to know,
And in their lord's advancement grow;
But in no memory were seen,
As under this, so straight and green;

8

Yet now no further strive to shoot,
Contented if they fix their root.
Nor to the wind's uncertain gust,
Their prudent heads too far entrust.   60
Only sometimes a fluttering breeze
Discourses with the breathing trees,
Which in their modest whispers name
Those acts that swelled the cheek of fame.

9

'Much other groves,' say they, 'than these
And other hills him once did please.
Through groves of pikes he thundered then,
And mountains raised of dying men.
For all the civic garlands due
To him, our branches are but few.   70
Nor are our trunks enow to bear
The trophies of one fertile year.'

10

'Tis true, ye trees, nor ever spoke
More certain oracles in oak.
But peace (if you his favour prize),
That courage its own praises flies.
Therefore to your obscurer seats
From his own brightness he retreats:

Nor he the hills without the groves,
Nor height, but with retirement, loves.   80

Upon Appleton House

To my Lord Fairfax

1

Within this sober frame expect
Work of no foreign architect,
That unto caves the quarries drew,
And forests did to pastures hew,
Who of his great design in pain
Did for a model vault his brain,
Whose columns should so high be raised
To arch the brows that on them gazed.

2

Why should of all things man unruled
Such unproportioned dwellings build?   10
The beasts are by their dens expressed:
And birds contrive an equal nest;
The low-roofed tortoises do dwell
In cases fit of tortoise shell:
No creature loves an empty space;
Their bodies measure out their place.

3

But he, superfluously spread,
Demands more room alive than dead;
And in his hollow palace goes
Where winds (as he) themselves may lose;   20
What need of all this marble crust
T'impark the wanton mote of dust,
That thinks by breadth the world t'unite
Though the first builders failed in height?

4

But all things are composèd here
Like Nature, orderly and near:
In which we the dimensions find
Of that more sober age and mind,
When larger-sizèd men did stoop
To enter at a narrow loop;   30
As practising, in doors so strait,
To strain themselves through heaven's gate.

5

And surely when the after age
Shall hither come in pilgrimage,
These sacred places to adore,
By Vere and Fairfax trod before,
Men will dispute how their extent
Within such dwarfish confines went:
And some will smile at this, as well
As Romulus his bee-like cell.   40

6

Humility alone designs
Those short but admirable lines,
By which, ungirt and unconstrained,
Things greater are in less contained.
Let others vainly strive t'immure
The circle in the quadrature!
These holy mathematics can
In every figure equal man.

7

Yet thus the laden house does sweat,
And scarce endures the master great: 50
But where he comes the swelling hall
Stirs, and the square grows spherical,
More by his magnitude distressed,
Then he is by its straitness pressed:
And too officiously it slights
That in itself which him delights.

8

So honour better lowness bears,
Than that unwonted greatness wears:
Height with a certain grace does bend,
But low things clownishly ascend.   60
And yet what needs there here excuse,
Where everything does answer use?
Where neatness nothing can condemn,
Nor pride invent what to contemn?

9

A stately frontispiece of poor
Adorns without the open door:
Nor less the rooms within commends
Daily new furniture of friends.
The house was built upon the place
Only as for a mark of grace;   70
And for an inn to entertain
Its Lord a while, but not remain.

10

Him Bishop's Hill or Denton may,
Or Bilbrough, better hold than they:
But Nature here hath been so free
As if she said, 'Leave this to me.'
Art would more neatly have defaced
What she had laid so sweetly waste,
In fragrant gardens, shady woods,
Deep meadows, and transparent floods.   80

11

While with slow eyes we these survey,
And on each pleasant footstep stay,
We opportunely may relate
The progress of this house's fate.
A nunnery first gave it birth
(For virgin buildings oft brought forth);
And all that neighbour-ruin shows
The quarries whence this dwelling rose.

12

Near to this gloomy cloister's gates
There dwelt the blooming virgin Thwaites,
Fair beyond measure, and an heir
Which might deformity make fair.
And oft she spent the summer suns
Discoursing with the subtle nuns.
Whence in these words one to her weaved,
(As 'twere by chance) thoughts long conceived.

13

'Within this holy leisure we
Live innocently, as you see.
These walls restrain the world without,
But hedge our liberty about.
These bars enclose that wider den
Of those wild creatures callèd men.
The cloister outward shuts its gates,
And, from us, locks on them the grates.

14

'Here we, in shining armour white,
Like virgin Amazons do fight.
And our chaste lamps we hourly trim,
Lest the great Bridegroom find them dim.
Our orient breaths perfumèd are
With incense of incessant prayer.
And holy-water of our tears
Most strangely our complexion clears.

15

'Not tears of grief; but such as those
With which calm pleasure overflows;
Or pity, when we look on you
That live without this happy vow.
How should we grieve that must be seen
Each one a spouse, and each a queen,
And can in heaven hence behold
Our brighter robes and crowns of gold?

16

'When we have prayèd all our beads,
Someone the holy legend reads;
While all the rest with needles paint
The face and graces of the saint.
But what the linen can't receive
They in their lives do interweave.
This work the saints best represents;
That serves for altar's ornaments.

17

'But much it to our work would add
If here your hand, your face we had: 130
By it we would Our Lady touch;
Yet thus she you resembles much.
Some of your features, as we sewed,
Through every shrine should be bestowed.
And in one beauty we would take
Enough a thousand saints to make.

18

'And (for I dare not quench the fire
That me does for your good inspire)
'Twere sacrilege a man t'admit
To holy things, for heaven fit.   140
I see the angels in a crown
On you the lilies showering down:
And round about you glory breaks,
That something more than human speaks.

19

'All beauty, when at such a height,
Is so already consecrate.
Fairfax I know; and long ere this
Have marked the youth, and what he is.
But can he such a rival seem
For whom you heav'n should disesteem?   150
Ah, no! and 'twould more honour prove
He your devoto were than love.

20

'Here live belovèd, and obeyed:
Each one your sister, each your maid.
And, if our rule seem strictly penned,
The rule itself to you shall bend.
Our abbess too, now far in age,
Doth your succession near presage.
How soft the yoke on us would lie,
Might such fair hands as yours it tie!   160

21

'Your voice, the sweetest of the choir,
Shall draw heaven nearer, raise us higher.
And your example, if our head,
Will soon us to perfection lead.
Those virtues to us all so dear,
Will straight grow sanctity when here:
And that, once sprung, increase so fast
Till miracles it work at last.

22

'Nor is our order yet so nice,
Delight to banish as a vice.   170
Here pleasure piety doth meet;
One pérfecting the other sweet.
So through the mortal fruit we boil
The sugar's uncorrupting oil:
And that which perished while we pull.
Is thus preservèd clear and full.

23

'For such indeed are all our arts,
Still handling Nature's finest parts.
Flowers dress the altars; for the clothes,
The sea-borne amber we compose;   180
Balms for the grieved we draw; and pastes
We mould, as baits for curious tastes.
What need is here of man? unless
These as sweet sins we should confess.

24

'Each night among us to your side
Appoint a fresh and virgin bride;
Whom if Our Lord at midnight find,
Yet neither should be left behind.
Where you may lie as chaste in bed,
As pearls together billeted,   190
All night embracing arm in arm
Like crystal pure with cotton warm.

25

'But what is this to all the store
Of joys you see, and may make more!
Try but a while, if you be wise:
The trial neither costs, nor ties.'
Now, Fairfax, seek her promised faith:
Religion that dispensèd hath,
Which she henceforward does begin;
The nun's smooth tongue has sucked her in.   200

26

Oft, though he knew it was in vain,
Yet would he valiantly complain.
'Is this that sanctity so great,
An art by which you finelier cheat?
Hypocrite witches, hence avaunt,
Who though in prison yet enchant!
Death only can such thieves make fast,
As rob though in the dungeon cast.

27

'Were there but, when this house was made,
One stone that a just hand had laid,   210
It must have fall'n upon her head
Who first thee from thy faith misled.
And yet, how well soever meant,
With them 'twould soon grow fraudulent:
For like themselves they alter all,
And vice infects the very wall.

28

'But sure those buildings last not long,
Founded by folly, kept by wrong.
I know what fruit their gardens yield,
When they it think by night concealed.   220
Fly from their vices. 'Tis thy 'state,
Not thee, that they would consecrate.
Fly from their ruin. How I fear,
Though guiltless, lest thou perish there.'

29

What should he do? He would respect
Religion, but not right neglect:
For first religion taught him right,
And dazzled not but cleared his sight.
Sometimes resolved, his sword he draws,
But reverenceth then the laws: 230
For justice still that courage led;
First from a judge, then soldier bred.

30

Small honour would be in the storm.
The court him grants the lawful form;
Which licensed either peace or force,
To hinder the unjust divorce.
Yet still the nuns his right debarred,
Standing upon their holy guard.
Ill-counselled women, do you know
Whom you resist, or what you do?   240

31

Is not this he whose offspring fierce
Shall fight through all the universe;
And with successive valour try
France, Poland, either Germany;
Till one, as long since prophesied,
His horse through conquered Britain ride?
Yet, against fate, his spouse they kept,
And the great race would intercept.

32

Some to the breach against their foes
Their wooden saints in vain oppose.   250
Another bolder stands at push
With their old holy-water brush.
While the disjointed abbess threads
The jingling chain-shot of her beads.
But their loudest cannon were their lungs;
And sharpest weapons were their tongues.

33

But waving these aside like flies,
Young Fairfax through the wall does rise.
Then th' unfrequented vault appeared,
And superstitions vainly feared.   260
The relics false were set to view;
Only the jewels there were true –
But truly bright and holy Thwaites
That weeping at the altar waits.

34

But the glad youth away her bears,
And to the nuns bequeaths her tears:
Who guiltily their prize bemoan,
Like gypsies that a child had stolen.
Thenceforth (as when th' enchantment ends,
The castle vanishes or rends)
The wasting cloister with the rest   270
Was in one instant dispossessed.

35

At the demolishing, this seat
To Fairfax fell as by escheat.
And what both nuns and founders willed
'Tis likely better thus fulfilled.
For if the virgin proved not theirs,
The cloister yet remainèd hers.
Though many a nun there made her vow,
'Twas no religious house till now.   280

36

From that blest bed the hero came,
Whom France and Poland yet does fame:
Who, when retirèd here to peace,
His warlike studies could not cease;
But laid these gardens out in sport
In the just figure of a fort;
And with five bastions it did fence,
As aiming one for every sense.

37

When in the east the morning ray
Hangs out the colours of the day,   290
The bee through these known alleys hums,
Beating the dian with its drums.
Then flowers their drowsy eyelids raise,
Their silken ensigns each displays,
And dries its pan yet dank with dew,
And fills its flask with odours new.

38

These, as their governor goes by,
In fragrant volleys they let fly;
And to salute their governess
Again as great a charge they press: 300
None for the virgin nymph; for she
Seems with the flowers a flower to be.
And think so still! though not compare
With breath so sweet, or cheek so fair.

39

Well shot, ye firemen! Oh how sweet,
And round your equal fires do meet,
Whose shrill report no ear can tell,
But echoes to the eye and smell.
See how the flowers, as at parade,
Under their colours stand displayed: 310
Each regiment in order grows,
That of the tulip, pink, and rose.

40

But when the vigilant patrol
Of stars walks round about the Pole,
Their leaves, that to the stalks are curled,
Seem to their staves the ensigns furled.
Then in some flower's belovèd hut
Each bee as sentinel is shut,
And sleep so too: but, if once stirred,
She runs you through, nor asks the word.   320

41

Oh thou, that dear and happy isle
The garden of the world ere while,
Thou paradise of foúr seas,
Which heaven planted us to please,
But, to exclude the world, did guard
With watery if not flaming sword;
What luckless apple did we taste,
To make us mortal, and thee waste?

42

Unhappy! shall we never more
That sweet militía restore,   330
When gardens only had their towers,
And all the garrisons were flowers,
When roses only arms might bear,
And men did rosy garlands wear?
Tulips, in several colours barred,
Were then the Switzers of our Guard.

43

The gardener had the soldier's place,
And his more gentle forts did trace.
The nursery of all things green
Was then the only magazine.   340
The winter quarters were the stoves,
Where he the tender plants removes.
But war all this doth overgrow;
We ordnance plant and powder sow.

44

And yet there walks one on the sod
Who, had it pleasèd him and God,
Might once have made our gardens spring
Fresh as his own and flourishing.
But he preferred to the Cinque Ports
These five imaginary forts,   350
And, in those half-dry trenches, spanned
Power which the ocean might command.

45

For he did, with his utmost skill,
Ambition weed, but conscience till –
Conscience, that heaven-nursèd plant,
Which most our earthy gardens want.
A prickling leaf it bears, and such
As that which shrinks at every touch;
But flowers eternal, and divine,
That in the crowns of saints do shine.   360

46

The sight does from these bastions ply,
The invisible artillery;
And at proud Cawood Castle seems
To point the battery of its beams.
As if it quarrelled in the seat
The ambition of its prelate great.
But o'er the meads below it plays,
Or innocently seems to graze.

47

And now to the abyss I pass
Of that unfathomable grass,   370
Where men like grasshoppers appear,
But grasshoppers are giants there:
They, in their squeaking laugh, contemn
Us as we walk more low than them:
And, from the precipices tall
Of the green spires, to us do call.

48

To see men through this meadow dive,
We wonder how they rise alive,
As, under water, none does know
Whether he fall through it or go.   380
But, as the mariners that sound,
And show upon their lead the ground,
They bring up flowers so to be seen,
And prove they've at the bottom been.

49

No scene that turns with engines strange
Does oftener than these meadows change.
For when the sun the grass hath vexed,
The tawny mowers enter next;
Who seem like Israelites to be,
Walking on foot through a green sea.   390
To them the grassy deeps divide,
And crowd a lane to either side.

50

With whistling scythe, and elbow strong,
These massacre the grass along:
While one, unknowing, carves the rail,
Whose yet unfeathered quills her fail.
The edge all bloody from its breast
He draws, and does his stroke detest,
Fearing the flesh untimely mowed
To him a fate as black forebode.   400

51

But bloody Thestylis, that waits
To bring the mowing camp their cates,
Greedy as kites, has trussed it up,
And forthwith means on it to sup:
When on another quick she lights,
And cries, 'He called us Israelites;
But now, to make his saying true,
Rails rain for quails, for manna, dew.'

52

Unhappy birds! what does it boot
To build below the grass's root;   410
When lowness is unsafe as height,
And chance o'ertakes, what 'scapeth spite?
And now your orphan parents' call
Sounds your untimely funeral.
Death-trumpets creak in such a note,
And 'tis the sourdine in their throat.

53

Or sooner hatch or higher build:
The mower now commands the field,
In whose new traverse seemeth wrought
A camp of battle newly fought: 420
Where, as the meads with hay, the plain
Lies quilted o'er with bodies slain:
The women that with forks it fling,
Do represent the pillaging.

54

And now the careless victors play,
Dancing the triumphs of the hay;
Where every mower's wholesome heat
Smells like an Alexander's sweat.
Their females fragrant as the mead
Which they in fairy circles tread: 430
When at their dance's end they kiss,
Their new-made hay not sweeter is.

55

When after this 'tis piled in cocks,
Like a calm sea it shows the rocks,
We wondering in the river near
How boats among them safely steer.
Or, like the desert Memphis sand,
Short pyramids of hay do stand.
And such the Roman camps do rise
In hills for soldiers' obsequies.   440

56

This scene again withdrawing brings
A new and empty face of things,
A levelled space, as smooth and plain
As cloths for Lely stretched to stain.
The world when first created sure
Was such a table rase and pure.
Or rather such is the *toril*
Ere the bulls enter at Madril.

57

For to this naked equal flat,
Which Levellers take pattern at,   450
The villagers in common chase
Their cattle, which it closer rase;
And what below the scythe increased
Is pinched yet nearer by the beast.
Such, in the painted world, appeared
D'Avenant with the universal herd.

58

They seem within the polished grass
A landskip drawn in looking-glass,
And shrunk in the huge pasture show
As spots, so shaped, on faces do –   460
Such fleas, ere they approach the eye,
In multiplying glasses lie.
They feed so wide, so slowly move,
As constellations do above.

59

Then, to conclude these pleasant acts,
Denton sets ope its cataracts,
And makes the meadow truly be
(What it but seemed before) a sea.
For, jealous of its Lord's long stay,
It tries t'invite him thus away.   470
The river in itself is drowned,
And isles th' astonished cattle round.

60

Let others tell the paradox,
How eels now bellow in the ox;
How horses at their tails do kick,
Turned as they hang to leeches quick;
How boats can over bridges sail;
And fishes do the stables scale.
How salmons trespassing are found;
And pikes are taken in the pound.   480

61

But I, retiring from the flood,
Take sanctuary in the wood,
And, while it lasts, myself embark
In this yet green, yet growing ark,
Where the first carpenter might best
Fit timber for his keel have pressed.
And where all creatures might have shares,
Although in armies, not in pairs.

62

The double wood of ancient stocks,
Linked in so thick, an union locks,   490
It like two pedigrees appears,
On th' one hand Fairfax, th' other Vere's:
Of whom though many fell in war,
Yet more to heaven shooting are:
And, as they Nature's cradle decked,
Will in green age her hearse expect.

63

When first the eye this forest sees
It seems indeed as wood not trees:
As if their neighbourhood so old
To one great trunk them all did mould.   500
There the huge bulk takes place, as meant
To thrust up a fifth element,
And stretches still so closely wedged
As if the night within were hedged.

64

Dark all without it knits; within
It opens passable and thin;
And in as loose an order grows,
As the Corinthian porticoes.
The arching boughs unite between
The columns of the temple green;   510
And underneath the wingèd choirs
Echo about their tunèd fires.

65

The nightingale does here make choice
To sing the trials of her voice.
Low shrubs she sits in, and adorns
With music high the squatted thorns.
But highest oaks stoop down to hear,
And listening elders prick the ear.
The thorn, lest it should hurt her, draws
Within the skin its shrunken claws.   520

66

But I have for my music found
A sadder, yet more pleasing sound:
The stock-doves, whose fair necks are graced
With nuptial rings, their ensigns chaste;
Yet always, for some cause unknown,
Sad pair unto the elms they moan.
O why should such a couple mourn,
That in so equal flames do burn!

67

Then as I careless on the bed
Of gelid strawberries do tread,   530
And through the hazels thick espy
The hatching throstles shining eye,
The heron from the ash's top,
The eldest of its young lets drop,
As if it stork-like did pretend
That tribute to its Lord to send.

68

But most the hewel's wonders are,
Who here has the holtfelster's care.
He walks still upright from the root,
Measuring the timber with his foot,   540
And all the way, to keep it clean,
Doth from the bark the woodmoths glean.
He, with his beak, examines well
Which fit to stand and which to fell.

69

The good he numbers up, and hacks,
As if he marked them with the axe.
But where he, tinkling with his beak,
Does find the hollow oak to speak,
That for his building he designs,
And through the tainted side he mines.   550
Who could have thought the tallest oak
Should fall by such a feeble stroke!

70

Nor would it, had the tree not fed
A traitor-worm, within it bred
(As first our flesh corrupt within
Tempts impotent and bashful sin).
And yet that worm triumphs not long,
But serves to feed the hewel's young,
While the oak seems to fall content,
Viewing the treason's punishment.   560

71

Thus I, easy philosopher,
Among the birds and trees confer.
And little now to make me wants
Or of the fowls, or of the plants:
Give me but wings as they, and I
Straight floating on the air shall fly:
Or turn me but, and you shall see
I was but an inverted tree.

72

Already I begin to call
In their most learn'd original: 570
And where I language want, my signs
The bird upon the bough divines;
And more attentive there doth sit
Than if she were with lime-twigs knit.
No leaf does tremble in the wind
Which I, returning, cannot find.

73

Out of these scattered sibyl's leaves
Strange prophecies my fancy weaves:
And in one history consumes,
Like Mexique paintings, all the plumes.   580
What Rome, Greece, Palestine, ere said
I in this light mosaic read.
Thrice happy he who, not mistook,
Hath read in Nature's mystic book.

74

And see how chance's better wit
Could with a mask my studies hit!
The oak leaves me embroider all,
Between which caterpillars crawl:
And ivy, with familiar trails,
Me licks, and clasps, and curls, and hales.   590
Under this antic cope I move
Like some great prelate of the grove.

75

Then, languishing with ease, I toss
On pallets swoll'n of velvet moss,
While the wind, cooling through the boughs,
Flatters with air my panting brows.
Thanks for my rest, ye mossy banks;
And unto you, cool zephyrs, thanks,
Who, as my hair, my thoughts too shed,
And winnow from the chaff my head.   600

76

How safe, methinks, and strong, behind
These trees have I encamped my mind:
Where beauty, aiming at the heart,
Bends in some tree its useless dart;
And where the world no certain shot
Can make, or me it toucheth not.
But I on it securely play,
And gall its horsemen all the day.

77

Bind me, ye woodbines, in your twines,
Curl me about, ye gadding vines,   610
And, oh, so close your circles lace,
That I may never leave this place:
But lest your fetters prove too weak,
Ere I your silken bondage break,
Do you, O brambles, chain me too,
And, courteous briars, nail me through.

78

Here in the morning tie my chain,
Where the two woods have made a lane,
While, like a guard on either side,
The trees before their Lord divide;   620
This, like a long and equal thread,
Betwixt two labyrinths does lead.
But where the floods did lately drown,
There at the evening stake me down.

79

For now the waves are fall'n and dried,
And now the meadows fresher dyed,
Whose grass, with moister colour dashed,
Seems as green silks but newly washed.
No serpent new nor crocodile
Remains behind our little Nile,   630
Unless itself you will mistake,
Among these meads the only snake.

80

See in what wanton harmless folds
It everywhere the meadow holds;
And its yet muddy back doth lick,
Till as a crystal mirror slick,
Where all things gaze themselves, and doubt
If they be in it or without.
And for his shade which therein shines,
Narcissus-like, the sun too pines.   640

81

O what a pleasure 'tis to hedge
My temples here with heavy sedge,
Abandoning my lazy side,
Stretched as a bank unto the tide,
Or to suspend my sliding foot
On th' osier's underminèd root,
And in its branches tough to hang,
While at my lines the fishes twang!

82

But now away my hooks, my quills,
And angles – idle utensíls.   650
The young Maria walks tonight:
Hide, trifling youth, thy pleasures slight.
'Twere shame that such judicious eyes
Should with such toys a man surprise;
She, that already is the law
Of all her sex, her age's awe.

83

See how loose Nature, in respect
To her, itself doth recollect;
And everything so whished and fine,
Starts forthwith to its *bonne mine*.   660
The sun himself, of her aware,
Seems to descend with greater care;
And lest she see him go to bed,
In blushing clouds conceals his head.

84

So when the shadows laid asleep
From underneath these banks do creep,
And on the river as it flows
With eben shuts begin to close;
The modest halcyon comes in sight,
Flying betwixt the day and night;   670
And such an horror calm and dumb,
Admiring Nature does benumb.

85

The viscous air, wheres'e'er she fly,
Follows and sucks her azure dye;
The jellying stream compacts below,
If it might fix her shadow so;
The stupid fishes hang, as plain
As flies in crystal overta'en;
And men the silent scene assist,
Charmed with the sapphire-wingèd mist.   680

86

Maria such, and so doth hush
The world, and through the evening rush.
No new-born comet such a train
Draws through the sky, nor star new-slain.
For straight those giddy rockets fail,
Which from the putrid earth exhale,
But by her flames, in heaven tried,
Nature is wholly vitrified.

87

'Tis she that to these gardens gave
That wondrous beauty which they have;   690
She straightness on the woods bestows;
To her the meadow sweetness owes;
Nothing could make the river be
So crystal pure but only she;
She yet more pure, sweet, straight, and fair,
Than gardens, woods, meads, rivers are.

88

Therefore what first she on them spent,
They gratefully again present:
The meadow, carpets where to tread;
The garden, flowers to crown her head;   700
And for a glass, the limpid brook,
Where she may all her beauties look;
But, since she would not have them seen,
The wood about her draws a screen.

89

For she, to higher beauties raised,
Disdains to be for lesser praised.
She counts her beauty to converse
In all the languages as hers;
Nor yet in those herself employs
But for the wisdom, not the noise;   710
Nor yet that wisdom would affect,
But as 'tis heaven's dialect.

90

Blest nymph! that couldst so soon prevent
Those trains by youth against thee meant:
Tears (watery shot that pierce the mind);
And signs (Love's cannon charged with wind);
True praise (that breaks through all defence);
And feigned complying innocence;
But knowing where this ambush lay,
She 'scaped the safe, but roughest way.   720

91

This 'tis to have been from the first
In a domestic heaven nursed,
Under the discipline severe
Of Fairfax, and the starry Vere;
Where not one object can come nigh
But pure, and spotless as the eye;
And goodness doth itself entail
On females, if there want a male.

92

Go now, fond sex, that on your face
Do all your useless study place, 730
Nor once at vice your brows dare knit
Lest the smooth forehead wrinkled sit:
Yet your own face shall at you grin,
Through the black-bag of your skin,
When knowledge only could have filled
And virtue all those furrows tilled.

93

Hence she with graces more divine
Supplies beyond her sex the line;
And like a sprig of mistletoe
On the Fairfacian oak does grow; 740
Whence, for some universal good,
The priest shall cut the sacred bud,
While her glad parents most rejoice,
And make their destiny their choice.

94

Meantime, ye fields, springs, bushes, flowers,
Where yet she leads her studious hours,
(Till fate her worthily translates,
And find a Fairfax for our Thwaites),
Employ the means you have by her,
And in your kind yourselves prefer; 750
That, as all virgins she precedes,
So you all woods, streams, gardens, meads.

95

For you, Thessalian Tempe's seat
Shall now be scorned as obsolete;
Aranjuez, as less, disdained;
The Bel-Retiro as constrained;
But name not the Idalian grove –
For 'twas the seat of wanton love –
Much less the dead's Elysian Fields,
Yet nor to them your beauty yields. 760

96

'Tis not, what once it was, the world,
But a rude heap together hurled,
All negligently overthrown,
Gulfs, deserts, precipices, stone.
Your lesser world contains the same,
But in more decent order tame;
You, heaven's centre, Nature's lap,
And paradise's only map.

97

But now the salmon-fishers moist
Their leathern boats begin to hoist,   770
And like Antipodes in shoes,
Have shod their heads in their canoes.
How tortoise-like, but not so slow,
These rational amphibii go!
Let's in: for the dark hemisphere
Does now like one of them appear.

The First Anniversary of the Government under His Highness the Lord Protector, 1655

Like the vain curlings of the watery maze,
Which in smooth streams a sinking weight does raise,
So man, declining always, disappears
In the weak circles of increasing years;
And his short tumults of themselves compose,
While flowing time above his head does close.
    Cromwell alone with greater vigour runs,
(Sun-like) the stages of succeeding suns:
And still the day which he doth next restore,
Is the just wonder of the day before.   10
Cromwell alone doth with new lustre spring,
And shines the jewel of the yearly ring.

'Tis he the force of scattered time contracts,
And in one year the work of ages acts:
While heavy monarchs make a wide return,
Longer, and more malignant than Saturn:
And though they all Platonic years should reign,
In the same posture would be found again.
Their earthy projects under ground they lay,
More slow and brittle than the China clay: 20
Well may they strive to leave them to their son,
For one thing never was by one king done.
Yet some more active for a frontier town,
Taken by proxy, beg a false renown;
Another triumphs at the public cost,
And will have won, if he no more have lost;
They fight by others, but in person wrong,
And only are against their subjects strong;
Their other wars seem but a feigned contést,
This common enemy is still oppressed;   30
If conquerors, on them they turn their might;
If conquered, on them they wreak their spite:
They neither build the temple in their days,
Nor matter for succeeding founders raise;
Nor sacred prophecies consult within,
Much less themself to pérfect them begin;
No other care they bear of things above,
But with astrologers divine of Jove
To know how long their planet yet reprieves
From the deservèd fate their guilty lives: 40
Thus (image-like) an useless time they tell,
And with vain sceptre strike the hourly bell,
Nor more contribute to the state of things,
Than wooden heads unto the viol's strings.
    While indefatigable Cromwell hies,
And cuts his way still nearer to the skies,
Learning a music in the region clear,
To tune this lower to that higher sphere.
    So when Amphion did the lute command,
Which the god gave him, with his gentle hand,   50
The rougher stones, unto his measures hewed,
Danced up in order from the quarries rude;
This took a lower, that an higher place,

As he the treble altered, or the bass:
No note he struck, but a new stone was laid,
And the great work ascended while he played.
   The listening structures he with wonder eyed,
And still new stops to various time applied:
Now through the strings a martial rage he throws,
And joining straight the Theban tower arose;   60
Then as he strokes them with a touch more sweet,
The flocking marbles in a palace meet;
But for he most the graver notes did try,
Therefore the temples reared their columns high:
Thus, ere he ceased, his sacred lute creates
Th' harmonious city of the seven gates.
   Such was that wondrous order and consent,
When Cromwell tuned the ruling Instrument,
While tedious statesmen many years did hack,
Framing a liberty that still went back,   70
Whose numerous gorge could swallow in an hour
That island, which the sea cannot devour:
Then our Amphion issues out and sings,
And once he struck, and twice, the powerful strings.
   The Commonwealth then first together came,
And each one entered in the willing frame;
All other matter yields, and may be ruled;
But who the minds of stubborn men can build?
No quarry bears a stone so hardly wrought,
Nor with such labour from its centre brought;   80
None to be sunk in the foundation bends,
Each in the house the highest place contends,
And each the hand that lays him will direct,
And some fall back upon the architect;
Yet all composed by his attractive song,
Into the animated city throng.
   The Commonwealth does through their centres all
Draw the circumference of the public wall;
The crossest spirits here do take their part,
Fastening the contignation which they thwart;   90
And they, whose nature leads them to divide,
Uphold this one, and that the other side;
But the most equal still sustain the height,
And they as pillars keep the work upright,

While the resistance of opposèd minds,
The fabric, as with arches, stronger binds,
Which on the basis of a senate free,
Knit by the roof's protecting weight, agree.
    When for his foot he thus a place had found,
He hurls e'er since the world about him round, 100
And in his several aspects, like a star,
Here shines in peace, and thither shoots in war,
While by his beams observing princes steer,
And wisely court the influence they fear.
O would they rather by his pattern won
Kiss the approaching, not yet angry Son;
And in their numbered footsteps humbly tread
The path where holy oracles do lead;
How might they under such a captain raise
The great designs kept for the latter days! 110
But mad with reason (so miscalled) of state
They know them not, and what they know not, hate.
Hence still they sing hosanna to the whore,
And her, whom they should massacre, adore:
But Indians, whom they should convert, subdue;
Nor teach, but traffic with, or burn the Jew.
    Unhappy princes, ignorantly bred,
By malice some, by error more misled,
If gracious heaven to my life give length,
Leisure to time, and to my weakness strength, 120
Then shall I once with graver accents shake
Your regal sloth, and your long slumbers wake:
Like the shrill huntsman that prevents the east,
Winding his horn to kings that chase the beast.
    Till then my muse shall hollo far behind
Angelic Cromwell who outwings the wind,
And in dark nights, and in cold days alone
Pursues the monster through every throne:
Which shrinking to her Roman den impure,
Gnashes her gory teeth; nor there secure. 130
    Hence oft I think if in some happy hour
High grace should meet in one with highest power,
And then a seasonable people still
Should bend to his, as he to heaven's will,

What we might hope, what wonderful effect
From such a wish'd conjuncture might reflect.
Sure, the mysterious work, where none withstand,
Would forthwith finish under such a hand:
Foreshortened time its useless course would stay,
And soon precipitate the latest day. 140
But a thick cloud about that morning lies,
And intercepts the beams of mortal eyes,
That 'tis the most which we determine can,
If these the times, then this must be the man.
And well he therefore does, and well has guessed,
Who in his age has always forward pressed:
And knowing not where heaven's choice may light,
Girds yet his sword, and ready stands to fight;
But men, alas, as if they nothing cared,
Look on, all unconcerned, or unprepared; 150
And stars still fall, and still the dragon's tail
Swinges the volumes of its horrid flail.
For the great justice that did first suspend
The world by sin, does by the same extend.
Hence that blest day still counterpoisèd wastes,
The ill delaying what th' elected hastes;
Hence landing nature to new seas is tossed,
And good designs still with their authors lost.
    And thou, great Cromwell, for whose happy birth
A mould was chosen out of better earth; 160
Whose saint-like mother we did lately see
Live out an age, long as a pedigree;
That she might seem (could we the Fall dispute),
T'have smelled the blossom, and not eat the fruit;
Though none does of more lasting parents grow,
Yet never any did them honour so,
Though thou thine heart from evil still unstained,
And always hast thy tongue from fraud refrained;
Thou, who so oft through storms of thundering lead
Hast born securely thine undaunted head, 170
Thy breast through poniarding conspiracies,
Drawn from the sheath of lying prophecies;
Thee proof beyond all other force or skill,
Our sins endanger, and shall one day kill.

How near they failed, and in thy sudden fall
At once assayed to overturn us all.
Our brutish fury struggling to be free,
Hurried thy horses while they hurried thee,
When thou hadst almost quit thy mortal cares,
And soiled in dust thy crown of silver hairs.   180
   Let this one sorrow interweave among
The other glories of our yearly song.
Like skilful looms, which through the costly thread
Of purling ore, a shining wave do shed:
So shall the tears we on past grief employ,
Still as they trickle, glitter in our joy.
So with more modesty we may be true,
And speak, as of the dead, the praises due:
While impious men deceived with pleasure short,
On their own hopes shall find the fall retort.   190
   But the poor beasts, wanting their noble guide,
(What could they more?) shrunk guiltily aside.
First wingèd fear transports them far away,
And leaden sorrow then their flight did stay.
See how they each his towering crest abate,
And the green grass, and their known mangers hate,
Nor through wide nostrils snuff the wanton air,
Nor their round hoofs, or curlèd manes compare;
With wandering eyes, and restless ears they stood,
And with shrill neighings asked him of the wood.   200
   Thou, Cromwell, falling, not a stupid tree,
Or rock so savage, but it mourned for thee:
And all about was heard a panic groan,
As if that Nature's self were overthrown.
It seemed the earth did from the centre tear;
It seemed the sun was fall'n out of the sphere:
Justice obstructed lay, and reason fooled;
Courage disheartened, and religion cooled.
A dismal silence through the palace went,
And then loud shrieks the vaulted marbles rent,   210
Such as the dying chorus sings by turns,
And to deaf seas, and ruthless tempests mourns,
When now they sink, and now the plundering streams
Break up each deck, and rip the oaken seams.

But thee triumphant hence the fiery car,
And fiery steeds had borne out of the war,
From the low world, and thankless men above,
Unto the kingdom blest of peace and love:
We only mourned ourselves, in thine ascent,
Whom thou hadst left beneath with mantle rent.   220

For all delight of life thou then didst lose,
When to command, thou didst thyself depose;
Resigning up thy privacy so dear,
To turn the headstrong people's charioteer;
For to be Cromwell was a greater thing,
Then ought below, or yet above a king:
Therefore thou rather didst thyself depress,
Yielding to rule, because it made thee less.

For neither didst thou from the first apply
Thy sober spirit unto things too high,   230
But in thine own fields exercised'st long,
An healthful mind within a body strong;
Till at the seventh time thou in the skies,
As a small cloud, like a man's hand, didst rise;
Then did thick mists and winds the air deform,
And down at last thou poured'st the fertile storm,
Which to the thirsty land did plenty bring,
But, though forewarned, o'ertook and wet the King.

What since he did, an higher force him pushed
Still from behind, and yet before him rushed,   240
Though undiscerned among the tumult blind,
Who think those high decrees by man designed.
'Twas heaven would not that his power should cease,
But walk still middle betwixt war and peace:
Choosing each stone, and poising every weight,
Trying the measures of the breadth and height;
Here pulling down, and there erecting new,
Founding a firm state by proportions true.

When Gideon so did from the war retreat,
Yet by the conquest of two kings grown great,   250
He on the peace extends a warlike power,
And Israel silent saw him raze the tower;
And how he Succoth's Elders durst suppress,
With thorns and briars of the wilderness.

No king might ever such a force have done;
Yet would not he be Lord, nor yet his son.
   Thou with the same strength, and an heart as plain,
Didst (like thine olive) still refuse to reign,
Though why should others all thy labour spoil,
And brambles be anointed with thine oil,   260
Whose climbing flame, without a timely stop,
Had quickly levelled every cedar's top?
Therefore first growing to thyself a law,
Th' ambitious shrubs thou in just time didst awe.
   So have I seen at sea, when whirling winds,
Hurry the bark, but more the seamen's minds,
Who with mistaken course salute the sand,
And threatening rocks misapprehend for land,
While baleful Tritons to the shipwreck guide,
And corposants along the tackling slide,   270
The passengers all wearied out before,
Giddy, and wishing for the fatal shore,
Some lusty mate, who with more careful eye
Counted the hours, and every star did spy,
The helm does from the artless steersman strain,
And doubles back unto the safer main.
What though a while they grumble discontent,
Saving himself, he does their loss prevent.
   'Tis not a freedom, that where all command;
Nor tyranny, where one does them withstand: 280
But who of both the bounders knows to lay
Him as their father must the state obey.
   Thou, and thine house (like Noah's eight) did rest,
Left by the wars' flood on the mountains' crest:
And the large vale lay subject to thy will,
Which thou but as an husbandman wouldst till:
And only didst for others plant the vine
Of liberty, not drunken with its wine.
   That sober liberty which men may have,
That they enjoy, but more they vainly crave: 290
And such as to their parents' tents do press,
May show their own, not see his nakedness.
   Yet such a Chammish issue still does rage,

The shame and plague both of the land and age,
Who watched thy halting, and thy fall deride,
Rejoicing when thy foot had slipped aside,
That their new king might the fifth sceptre shake,
And make the world, by his example, quake:
Whose frantic army should they want for men
Might muster heresies, so one were ten.   300
What thy misfortune, they the spirit call,
And their religion only is to fall.
Oh Mahomet! now couldst thou rise again,
Thy falling-sickness should have made thee reign,
While Feake and Simpson would in many a tome,
Have writ the comments of thy sacred foam:
For soon thou mightst have passed among their rant
Were't but for thine unmovèd tulipant;
As thou must needs have owned them of thy band
For prophecies fit to be Al-Koraned.   310

   Accursèd locusts, whom your king does spit
Out of the centre of th' unbottomed pit;
Wanderers, adulterers, liars, Münster's rest,
Sorcerers, atheists, Jesuits possessed;
You who the scriptures and the laws deface
With the same liberty as points and lace;
Oh race most hypocritically strict!
Bent to reduce us to the ancient Pict;
Well may you act the Adam and the Eve;
Ay, and the serpent too that did deceive.   320

   But the great captain, now the danger's o'er,
Makes you for his sake tremble one fit more;
And, to your spite, returning yet alive
Does with himself all that is good revive.

   So when first man did through the morning new
See the bright sun his shining race pursue,
All day he followed with unwearied sight,
Pleased with that other world of moving light;
But thought him when he missed his setting beams,
Sunk in the hills, or plunged below the streams.   330

While dismal blacks hung round the universe,
And stars (like tapers) burned upon his hearse:
And owls and ravens with their screeching noise
Did make the funerals sadder by their joys.
His weeping eyes the doleful vigils keep,
Not knowing yet the night was made for sleep:
Still to the west, where he him lost, he turned,
And with such accents as despairing mourned:
'Why did mine eyes once see so bright a ray;
Or why day last no longer than a day?'   340
When straight the sun behind him he descried,
Smiling serenely from the further side.

    So while our star that gives us light and heat,
Seemed now a long and gloomy night to threat,
Up from the other world his flame he darts,
And princes (shining through their windows) starts,
Who their suspected counsellors refuse,
And credulous ambassadors accuse.

    'Is this,' saith one, 'the nation that we read
Spent with both wars, under a captain dead,   350
Yet rig a navy while we dress us late,
And ere we dine, raze and rebuild their state?
What oaken forests, and what golden mines!
What mints of men, what union of designs!
(Unless their ships, do, as their fowl proceed
Of shedding leaves, that with their ocean breed).
Theirs are not ships, but rather arks of war
And beakèd promontories sailed from far;
Of floating islands a new hatchèd nest;
A fleet of worlds, of other worlds in quest;   360
An hideous shoal of wood-leviathans,
Armed with three tier of brazen hurricanes,
That through the centre shoot their thundering side
And sink the earth that does at anchor ride.
What refuge to escape them can be found,
Whose watery leaguers all the world surround?
Needs must we all their tributaries be,

Whose navies hold the sluices of the sea.
The ocean is the fountain of command,
But that once took, we captives are on land.   370
And those that have the waters for their share,
Can quickly leave us neither earth nor air.
Yet if through these our fears could find a pass,
Through double oak, and lined with treble brass,
That one man still, although but named, alarms
More than all men, all navies, and all arms.
Him, in the day, him, in late night I dread,
And still his sword seems hanging o'er my head.
The nation had been ours, but his one soul
Moves the great bulk, and animates the whole.   380
He secrecy with number hath enchased,
Courage with age, maturity with haste:
The valiant's terror, riddle of the wise,
And still his falchion all our knots unties.
Where did he learn those arts that cost us dear?
Where below earth, or where above the sphere?
He seems a king by long succession born,
And yet the same to be a king does scorn.
Abroad a king he seems, and something more,
At home a subject on the equal floor.   390
O could I once him with our title see,
So should I hope that he might die as we.
But let them write his praise that love him best,
It grieves me sore to have thus much confessed.'
    Pardon, great Prince, if thus their fear or spite
More than our love and duty do thee right.
I yield, nor further will the prize contend,
So that we both alike may miss our end:
While thou thy venerable head dost raise
As far above their malice as my praise,   400
And as the Angel of our commonweal,
Troubling the waters, yearly mak'st them heal.

A Poem upon the Death of
His Late Highness the Lord Protector

That Providence which had so long the care
Of Cromwell's head, and numbered every hair,
Now in itself (the glass where all appears)
Had seen the period of his golden years:
And thenceforth only did attend to trace
What death might least so fair a life deface.
   The people, which what most they fear esteem,
Death when more horrid, so more noble deem,
And blame the last act, like spectators vain,
Unless the prince whom they applaud be slain.   10
Nor fate indeed can well refuse that right
To those that lived in war, to die in fight.
   But long his valour none had left that could
Endanger him, or clemency that would.
And he whom Nature all for peace had made,
But angry heaven unto war had swayed,
And so less useful where he most desired,
For what he least affected was admired,
Deservèd yet an end whose every part,
Should speak the wondrous softness of his heart.   20
   To Love and Grief the fatal writ was 'signed;
(Those nobler weaknesses of human kind,
From which those powers that issued the decree,
Although immortal, found they were not free),
That they, to whom his breast still open lies,
In gentle passions should his death disguise:
And leave succeeding ages cause to mourn,
As long as Grief shall weep, or Love shall burn.
   Straight does a slow and languishing disease
Eliza, Nature's and his darling, seize.   30
Her when an infant, taken with her charms,
He oft would flourish in his mighty arms,
And, lest their force the tender burden wrong,
Slacken the vigour of his muscles strong;
Then to the Mother's breast her softly move,

Which while she drained of milk, she filled with love.
But as with riper years her virtue grew,
And every minute adds a lustre new,
When with meridian height her beauty shined,
And thorough that sparkled her fairer mind,   40
When she with smiles serene in words discreet
His hidden soul at every turn could meet;
Then might y'ha' daily his affection spied,
Doubling that knot which destiny had tied,
While they by sense, not knowing, comprehend
How on each other both their fates depend.
With her each day the pleasing hours he shares,
And at her aspect calms his growing cares;
Or with a grandsire's joy her children sees
Hanging about her neck or at his knees.   50
Hold fast, dear infants, hold them both or none;
This will not stay when once the other's gone.
    A silent fire now wastes those limbs of wax,
And him within his tortured image racks.
So the flower withering which the garden crowned,
The sad root pines in secret under ground.
Each groan he doubled and each sigh he sighed,
Repeated over to the restless night.
No trembling string composed to numbers new,
Answers the touch in notes more sad, more true.   60
She, lest he grieve, hides what she can her pains,
And he to lessen hers his sorrow feigns:
Yet both perceived, yet both concealed their skills,
And so diminishing increased their ills:
That whether by each other's grief they fell,
Or on their own redoubled, none can tell.
    And now Eliza's purple locks were shorn,
Where she so long her Father's fate had worn:
And frequent lightning to her soul that flies,
Divides the air, and opens all the skies: 70
And now his life, suspended by her breath,
Ran out impetuously to hasting death.
Like polished mirrors, so his steely breast
Had every figure of her woes expressed,
And with the damp of her last gasp obscured,

Had drawn such stains as were not to be cured.
Fate could not either reach with single stroke,
But the dear image fled, the mirror broke.
    Who now shall tell us more of mournful swans,
Of halcyons kind, or bleeding pelicans?   80
No downy breast did e'er so gently beat,
Or fan with airy plumes so soft an heat.
For he no duty by his height excused,
Nor, though a prince, to be a man refused:
But rather than in his Eliza's pain
Not love, not grieve, would neither live nor reign:
And in himself so oft immortal tried,
Yet in compassion of another died.
    So have I seen a vine, whose lasting age
Of many a winter hath survived the rage,   90
Under whose shady tent men every year
At its rich blood's expense their sorrow cheer,
If some dear branch where it extends its life
Chance to be pruned by an untimely knife,
The parent-tree unto the grief succeeds,
And through the wound its vital humour bleeds,
Trickling in watery drops, whose flowing shape
Weeps that it falls ere fixed into a grape.
So the dry stock, no more that spreading vine,
Frustrates the autumn and the hopes of wine.   100
    A secret cause does sure those signs ordain
Foreboding princes' falls, and seldom vain.
Whether some kinder powers that wish us well,
What they above cannot prevent foretell;
Or the great world do by consent presage,
As hollow seas with future tempests rage;
Or rather heaven, which us so long foresees,
Their funerals celebrates while it decrees.
But never yet was any human fate
By Nature solemnised with so much state.   110
He unconcerned the dreadful passage crossed;
But, oh, what pangs that death did Nature cost!
    First the great thunder was shot off, and sent
The signal from the starry battlement.
The winds receive it, and its force outdo,

As practising how they could thunder too;
Out of the binder's hand the sheaves they tore,
And thrashed the harvest in the airy floor;
Or of huge trees, whose growth with his did rise,
The deep foundations opened to the skies.   120
Then heavy showers the wingèd tempests lead,
And pour the deluge o'er the chaos' head.
The race of warlike horses at his tomb
Offer themselves in many a hecatomb;
With pensive head towards the ground they fall,
And helpless languish at the tainted stall.
Numbers of men decrease with pains unknown,
And hasten, not to see his death, their own.
Such tortures all the elements unfixed,
Troubled to part where so exactly mixed.   130
And as through air his wasting spirits flowed,
The universe laboured beneath their load.
     Nature, it seemed with him would Nature vie;
He with Eliza, it with him would die.
     He without noise still travelled to his end,
As silent suns to meet the night descend.
The stars that for him fought had only power
Left to determine now his fatal hour,
Which, since they might not hinder, yet they cast
To choose it worthy of his glories past.   140
     No part of time but bare his mark away
Of honour; all the year was Cromwell's day:
But this, of all the most auspicious found,
Twice had in open field him victor crowned:
When up the armèd mountains of Dunbar
He marched, and through deep Severn ending war.
What day should him eternise but the same
That had before immortalised his name?
That so who ere would at his death have joyed,
In their own griefs might find themselves employed;   150
But those that sadly his departure grieved,
Yet joyed, remembering what he once achieved.
And the last minute his victorious ghost
Gave chase to Ligny on the Belgic coast.
Here ended all his mortal toils: he laid

And slept in peace under the laurel shade.
  O Cromwell, heaven's favourite! To none
Have such high honours from above been shown:
For whom the elements we mourners see,
And heaven itself would the great herald be,   160
Which with more care set forth his obsequies
Than those of Moses hid from human eyes,
As jealous only here lest all be less,
That we could to his memory express.
  Then let us to our course of mourning keep:
Where heaven leads, 'tis piety to weep.
Stand back, ye seas, and shrunk beneath the veil
Of your abyss, with covered head bewail
Your monarch: we demand not your supplies
To compass in our isle; our tears suffice: 170
Since him away the dismal tempest rent,
Who once more joined us to the continent;
Who planted England on the Flandric shore,
And stretched our frontier to the Indian ore;
Whose greater truths obscure the fables old,
Whether of British saints or worthies told;
And in a valour lessening Arthur's deeds,
For holiness the Confessor exceeds.
  He first put arms into Religion's hand,
And timorous Conscience unto Courage manned: 180
The soldier taught that inward mail to wear,
And fearing God how they should nothing fear.
'Those strokes,' he said, 'will pierce through all below
Where those that strike from heaven fetch their blow.'
Astonished armies did their flight prepare,
And cities strong were stormèd by his prayer;
Of that, forever Preston's field shall tell
The story, and impregnable Clonmel.
And where the sandy mountain Fenwick scaled,
The sea between, yet hence his prayer prevailed.   190
What man was ever so in heaven obeyed
Since the commanded sun o'er Gibeon stayed?
In all his wars needs must he triumph when
He conquered God still ere he fought with men:
  Hence, though in battle none so brave or fierce,

Yet him the adverse steel could never pierce.
Pity it seemed to hurt him more that felt
Each wound himself which he to others dealt;
Danger itself refusing to offend
So loose an enemy, so fast a friend.   200
    Friendship, that sacred virtue, long does claim
The first foundation of his house and name:
But within one its narrow limits fall,
His tenderness extended unto all.
And that deep soul through every channel flows,
Where kindly nature loves itself to lose.
More strong affections never reason served,
Yet still affected most what best deserved.
If he Eliza loved to that degree,
(Though who more worthy to be loved than she?)   210
If so indulgent to his own, how dear
To him the children of the Highest were?
For her he once did nature's tribute pay:
For these his life adventured every day:
And 'twould be found, could we his thoughts have cast,
Their griefs struck deepest, if Eliza's last.
    What prudence more than human did he need
To keep so dear, so differing minds agreed?
The worser sort, as conscious of their ill,
Lie weak and easy to the ruler's will;   220
But to the good (too many or too few)
All law is useless, all reward is due.
Oh ill-advised, if not for love, for shame,
Spare yet your own, if you neglect his fame;
Lest others dare to think your zeal a mask,
And you to govern, only heaven's task.
    Valour, religion, friendship, prudence died
At once with him, and all that's good beside;
And we death's refuse, nature's dregs, confined
To loathsome life, alas, are left behind!   230
Where we (so once we used) shall now no more
To fetch day, press about his chamber door
From which he issued with that awful state,
It seemed Mars broke through Janus' double gate,
Yet always tempered with an air so mild,

No April suns that e'er so gently smiled;
No more shall hear that powerful language charm,
Whose force oft spared the labour of his arm:
No more shall follow where he spent the days
In war, in counsel, or in prayer and praise,   240
Whose meanest acts he would himself advance,
As ungirt David to the ark did dance.
All, all is gone of ours or his delight
In horses fierce, wild deer, or armour bright;
Francisca fair can nothing now but weep,
Nor with soft notes shall sing his cares asleep.
    I saw him dead. A leaden slumber lies
And mortal sleep over those wakeful eyes:
Those gentle rays under the lids were fled,
Which through his looks that piercing sweetness shed;   250
That port which so majestic was and strong,
Loose and deprived of vigour, stretched along:
All withered, all discoloured, pale and wan –
How much another thing, nor more that man?
O human glory vain, O death, O wings,
O worthless world, O transitory things!
    Yet dwelt that greatness in his shape decayed,
That still, though dead, greater than death he laid;
And in his altered face you something feign
That threatens death he yet will live again.   260
    Not much unlike the sacred oak which shoots
To heaven its branches and through earth its roots,
Whose spacious boughs are hung with trophies round,
And honoured wreaths have oft the victor crowned.
When angry Jove darts lightning through the air,
At mortals' sins, nor his own plant will spare
(It groans, and bruises all below, that stood
So many years the shelter of the wood),
The tree erewhile foreshortened to our view,
When fall'n shows taller yet than as it grew: 270
    So shall his praise to after times increase,
When truth shall be allowed, and faction cease,
And his own shadows with him fall. The eye
Detracts from objects than itself more high:

But when death takes them from that envied seat,
Seeing how little, we confess how great.
    Thee, many ages hence in martial verse
Shall the English soldier, ere he charge, rehearse,
Singing of thee, inflame themselves to fight,
And with the name of Cromwell, armies fright.   280
As long as rivers to the seas shall run,
As long as Cynthia shall relieve the sun,
While stags shall fly unto the forests thick,
While sheep delight the grassy downs to pick,
As long as future times succeeds the past,
Always thy honour, praise, and name shall last.
    Thou in a pitch how far beyond the sphere
Of human glory tower'st, and reigning there
Despoiled of mortal robes, in seas of bliss,
Plunging dost bathe, and tread the bright abyss: 290
There thy great soul at once a world does see,
Spacious enough, and pure enough for thee.
How soon thou Moses hast, and Joshua found,
And David for the sword and harp renowned!
How straight canst to each happy mansion go!
(Far better known above than here below)
And in those joys dost spend the endless day,
Which in expressing we ourselves betray.
    For we, since thou art gone, with heavy doom,
Wander like ghosts about thy lovèd tomb;   300
And lost in tears, have neither sight nor mind
To guide us upward through this region blind.
Since thou art gone, who best that way couldst teach,
Only our sighs, perhaps, may thither reach.
    And Richard yet, where his great parent led,
Beats on the rugged track: he, virtue dead,
Revives, and by his milder beams assures;
And yet how much of them his grief obscures?
    He, as his father, long was kept from sight
In private, to be viewed by better light;   310
But opened once, what splendour does he throw:

A Cromwell in an hour a prince will grow!
How he becomes that seat, how strongly strains,
How gently winds at once the ruling reins?
Heaven to this choice prepared a diadem,
Richer than any Eastern silk or gem;
A pearly rainbow, where the sun enchased
His brows, like an imperial jewel graced.
   We find already what those omens mean,
Earth ne'er more glad, nor heaven more serene.   320
Cease now our griefs, calm peace succeeds a war,
Rainbows to storms, Richard to Oliver.
Tempt not his clemency to try his power,
He threats no deluge, yet foretells a shower.

Flecknoe, an English Priest at Rome

Obliged by frequent visits of this man,
Whom as priest, poet, and musícian,
I for some branch of Melchizédek took
(Though he derives himself from my Lord Brooke);
I sought his lodging, which is at the sign
Of The Sad Pelican – subject divine
For poetry. There, three staircases high,
Which signifies his triple property,
I found at last a chamber, as 'twas said,
But seemed a coffin set on the stairs' head   10
Not higher than seven, nor larger than three feet;
Only there was nor ceiling, nor a sheet,
Save that th' ingenious door did, as you come,
Turn in, and show to wainscot half the room.
Yet of his state no man could have complained,
There being no bed where he entertained:
And though within one cell so narrow pent,

He'd stanzas for a whole appartement.
    Straight, without further information,
In hideous verse, he, in a dismal tone,   20
Begins to exorcise, as if I were
Possessed; and sure the Devil brought me there.
But I, who now imagined myself brought
To my last trial, in a serious thought
Calmed the disorders of my youthful breast,
And to my martyrdom preparèd rest.
Only this frail ambition did remain,
The last distemper of the sober brain,
That there had been some present to assure
The future ages how I did endure: 30
And how I, silent, turned my burning ear
Towards the verse; and when that could not hear,
Held him the other; and unchangèd yet,
Asked still for more, and prayed him to repeat:
Till the tyrant, weary to persecute,
Left off, and tried t' allure me with his lute.
    Now as two instruments, to the same key
Being tuned by art, if the one touchèd be
The other opposite as soon replies,
Moved by the air and hidden sympathies;   40
So while he with his gouty fingers crawls
Over the lute, his murm'ring belly calls,
Whose hungry guts to the same straitness twined
In echo to the trembling strings repined.
    I, that perceived now what his music meant,
Asked civilly if he had eat this Lent.
He answered yes, with such and such an one.
For he has this of generous, that alone
He never feeds, save only when he tries
With gristly tongue to dart the passing flies.   50
I asked if he eat flesh. And he, that was
So hungry that, though ready to say Mass,
Would break his fast before, said he was sick,
And the ordinance was only politic.

Nor was I longer to invite him scant,
Happy at once to make him Protestant,
And silent. Nothing now our dinner stayed
But till he had himself a body made –
I mean till he were dressed: for else so thin
He stands, as if he only fed had been   60
With consecrated wafers: and the Host
Hath sure more flesh and blood than he can boast.
This *basso rilievo* of a man,
Who as a camel tall, yet easily can
The needle's eye thread without any stitch
(His only impossible is to be rich),
Lest his too subtle body, growing rare,
Should leave his soul to wander in the air,
He therefore circumscribes himself in rhymes;
And swaddled in's own papers seven times,   70
Wears a close jacket of poetic buff,
With which he doth his third dimension stuff.
Thus armèd underneath, he over all
Does make a primitive *sottana* fall;
And above that yet casts an antique cloak,
Torn at the first Council of Antioch,
Which by the Jews long hid, and disesteemed,
He heard of by tradition, and redeemed.
But were he not in this black habit decked,
This half-transparent man would soon reflect   80
Each colour that he passed by, and be seen,
As the chameleon, yellow, blue, or green.

He dressed, and ready to disfurnish now
His chamber, whose compactness did allow
No empty place for complimenting doubt,
But who came last is forced first to go out;
I meet one on the stairs who made me stand,
Stopping the passage, and did him demand.
I answered, 'He is here, Sir; but you see
You cannot pass to him but thorough me.'   90
He thought himself affronted, and replied,
'I whom the palace never has denied
Will make the way here'; I said, 'Sir, you'll do

Me a great favour, for I seek to go.'
He gathering fury still made sign to draw;
But himself there closed in a scabbard saw
As narrow as his sword's; and I, that was
Delightful, said, 'There can no body pass
Except by penetration hither, where
Two make a crowd; nor can three persons here   100
Consist but in one substance.' Then, to fit
Our peace, the priest said I too had some wit.
To prov't, I said, 'The place doth us invite
By its own narrowness, Sir, to unite.'
He asked me pardon; and to make me way
Went down, as I him followed to obey.
But the propitiatory priest had straight
Obliged us, when below, to celebrate
Together our atonement: so increased
Betwixt us two the dinner to a feast.   110
  Let it suffice that we could eat in peace;
And that both poems did and quarrels cease
During the table; though my new-made friend
Did, as he threatened, ere 'twere long intend
To be both witty and valiant: I, loath,
Said 'twas too late, he was already both.
  But now, alas, my first tormentor came,
Who satisfied with eating, but not tame,
Turns to recite; though judges most severe
After th' Assizes' dinner mild appear,   120
And on full stomach do condemn but few,
Yet he more strict my sentence doth renew,
And draws out of the black box of his breast
Ten quire of paper in which he was dressed.
Yet that which was a greater cruelty
Than Nero's poem, he calls charity:
And so the pelican at his door hung
Picks out the tender bosom to its young.
  Of all his poems there he stands ungirt
Save only two foul copies for his shirt: 130

Yet these he promises as soon as clean.
But how I loathed to see my neighbour glean
Those papers which he peelèd from within
Like white flakes rising from a leper's skin!
More odious than those rags which the French youth
At ordinaries after dinner show'th
When they compare their chancres and poulains.
Yet he first kissed them, and after takes pains
To read; and then, because he understood
Not one word, thought and swore that they were good.   140
But all his praises could not now appease
The provoked author, whom it did displease
To hear his verses, by so just a curse,
That were ill made, condemned to be read worse:
And how (impossible) he made yet more
Absurdities in them than were before.
For he his untuned voice did fall or raise
As a deaf man upon a viol plays,
Making the half points and the periods run
Confuseder than the atoms in the sun.   150
Thereat the poet swelled, with anger full,
And roared out, like Perillus in's own bull:
'Sir, you read false.' 'That, any one but you,
Should know the contrary.' Whereat, I, now
Made mediator, in my room, said, 'Why,
To say that you read false, Sir, is no lie.'
Thereat the waxen youth relented straight;
But saw with sad despair that 'twas too late.
For the disdainful poet was retired
Home, his most furious satire to have fired   160
Against the rebel, who, at this struck dead,
Wept bitterly as disinherited.
Who should commend his mistress now? Or who
Praise him? Both difficult indeed to do
With truth. I counselled him to go in time,
Ere the fierce poet's anger turned to rhyme.
    He hasted; and I, finding myself free,
As one 'scaped strangely from captivity,

Have made the chance be painted; and go now
To hang it in Saint Peter's for a vow.   170

To his Noble Friend Mr Richard Lovelace, upon his Poems

Sir,
Our times are much degenerate from those
Which your sweet muse with your fair fortune chose,
And as complexions alter with the climes,
Our wits have drawn the infection of our times.
That candid age no other way could tell
To be ingenious, but by speaking well.
Who best could praise had then the greatest praise,
'Twas more esteemed to give than wear the bays:
Modest ambition studied only then
To honour not herself but worthy men.   10
These virtues now are banished out of town,
Our civil wars have lost the civic crown.
He highest builds, who with most art destroys,
And against others' fame his own employs.
I see the envious caterpillar sit
On the fair blossom of each growing wit.
    The air's already tainted with the swarms
Of insects which against you rise in arms:
Word-peckers, paper-rats, book-scorpions,
Of wit corrupted, the unfashioned sons.   20
The barbèd censurers begin to look
Like the grim consistory on thy book;
And on each line cast a reforming eye,
Severer than the young presbýtery.

Till when in vain they have thee all perused,
You shall, for being faultless, be accused.
Some reading your *Lucasta* will allege
You wronged in her the House's privilege.
Some that you under sequestration are,
Because you writ when going to the war,   30
And one the book prohibits, because Kent
Their first petition by the author sent.
   But when the beauteous ladies came to know
That their dear Lovelace was endangered so:
Lovelace that thawed the most congealèd breast,
He who loved best and them defended best,
Whose hand so rudely grasps the steely brand,
Whose hand so gently melts the lady's hand,
They all in mutiny though yet undressed
Sallied, and would in his defence contest.   40
And one, the loveliest that was yet e'er seen,
Thinking that I too of the rout had been,
Mine eyes invaded with a female spite,
(She knew what pain 'twould be to lose that sight.)
'O no, mistake not,' I replied, 'for I
In your defence, or in his cause, would die.'
But he, secure of glory and of time,
Above their envy, or mine aid, doth climb.
Him valiant'st men and fairest nymphs approve;
His book in them finds judgement, with you love.   50

Tom May's Death

As one put drunk into the packet-boat,
Tom May was hurried hence and did not know't.
But was amazèd on th' Elysian side,
And with an eye uncertain, gazing wide,
Could not determine in what place he was,
(For whence, in Stephen's Alley, trees or grass?)
Nor where The Pope's Head, nor The Mitre lay,

Signs by which still he found and lost his way.
At last while doubtfully he all compares,
He saw near hand, as he imagined, Ayres.   10
Such did he seem for corpulence and port,
But 'twas a man much of another sort;
'Twas Ben that in the dusky laurel shade
Amongst the chorus of old poets layed,
Sounding of ancient heroes, such as were
The subjects' safety, and the rebels' fear,
And how a double-headed vulture eats
Brutus and Cassius, the people's cheats.
But seeing May, he varied straight his song,
Gently to signify that he was wrong.   20
'Cups more than civil of Emathian wine,
I sing' (said he) 'and the Pharsalian Sign,
Where the historian of the commonwealth
In his own bowels sheathed the conquering health.'
By this, May to himself and them was come,
He found he was translated, and by whom,
Yet then with foot as stumbling as his tongue
Pressed for his place among the learned throng.
But Ben, who knew not neither foe nor friend,
Sworn enemy to all that do pretend,   30
Rose; more than ever he was seen severe,
Shook his grey locks, and his own bays did tear
At this intrusion. Then with laurel wand
(The awful sign of his supreme command,
At whose dread whisk Virgil himself does quake,
And Horace patiently its stroke does take)
As he crowds in, he whipped him o'er the pate
Like Pembroke at the masque, and then did rate:
    'Far from these blessed shades tread back again
Most servile wit, and mercenary pen,   40
Polydore, Lucan, Alan, Vandal, Goth,
Malignant poet and historian both,
Go seek the novice statesmen, and obtrude
On them some Roman-cast similitude,
Tell them of liberty, the stories fine,
Until you all grow consuls in your wine;
Or thou, dictator of the glass, bestow

On him the Cato, this the Cicero,
Transferring old Rome hither in your talk,
As Bethlem's House did to Loreto walk.   50
Foul architect, that hadst not eye to see
How ill the measures of these states agree,
And who by Rome's example England lay,
Those but to Lucan do continue May.
But thee nor ignorance nor seeming good
Misled, but malice fixed and understood.
Because some one than thee more worthy wears
The sacred laurel, hence are all these tears?
Must therefore all the world be set on flame,
Because a gázette-writer missed his aim?   60
And for a tankard-bearing muse must we
As for the basket, Guelphs and Ghib'llines be?
When the sword glitters o'er the judge's head,
And fear has coward churchmen silencèd,
Then is the poet's time, 'tis then he draws,
And single fights forsaken virtue's cause.
He, when the wheel of empire whirleth back,
And though the world's disjointed axle crack,
Sings still of ancient rights and better times,
Seeks wretched good, arraigns successful crimes.   70
But thou, base man, first prostituted hast
Our spotless knowledge and the studies chaste,
Apostatising from our arts and us,
To turn the chronicler to Spartacus.
Yet wast thou taken hence with equal fate,
Before thou couldst great Charles his death relate.
But what will deeper wound thy little mind,
Hast left surviving D'Avenant still behind,
Who laughs to see in this thy death renewed,
Right Roman poverty and gratitude.   80
Poor poet thou, and grateful senate they,
Who thy last reckoning did so largely pay,
And with the public gravity would come,
When thou hadst drunk thy last to lead thee home,
If that can be thy home where Spenser lies,
And reverend Chaucer, but their dust does rise
Against thee, and expels thee from their side,

As th' eagle's plumes from other birds divide.
Nor here thy shade must dwell. Return, return,
Where sulphury Phlegethon does ever burn. 90
Thee Cerberus with all his jaws shall gnash,
Megaera thee with all her serpents lash.
Thou riveted unto Ixíon's wheel
Shalt break, and the perpetual vulture feel.
'Tis just, what torments poets e'er did feign,
Thou first historically shouldst sustain.'
    Thus, by irrevocable sentence cast,
May, only Master of these Revels, passed.
And straight he vanished in a cloud of pitch,
Such as unto the Sabbath bears the witch. 100

An Epitaph upon Frances Jones

Enough: and leave the rest to fame.
'Tis to commend her but to name.
Courtship, which living she declined,
When dead to offer were unkind.
Where never any could speak ill,
Who would officious praises spill?
Nor can the truest wit or friend,
Without detracting, her commend.
To say she lived a virgin chaste,
In this age loose and all unlaced; 10
Nor was, when vice is so allowed,
Of virtue or ashamed, or proud;
That her soul was on heav'n so bent
No minute but it came and went;
That ready her last debt to pay
She summed her life up every day;
Modest as morn; as midday bright;
Gentle as evening; cool as night;
'Tis true: but all so weakly said,
'Twere more significant, she's dead. 20

Notes

p.3 *A Dialogue between the Resolved Soul and Created Pleasure*
Resolved: resolute. **l.18 bait:** refresh. **l.39 posting:** hastening.
l.71 centre: centre of the earth.

p.6 *On a Drop of Dew* **l.1 orient:** shining like a pearl. **l.3 blowing:**
blossoming. **l.5 For:** because of. **l.27 coy:** modest. **l.34 girt:** prepared.
l.37 Such: so.

p.7 *The Coronet* **l.7 towers:** head-dresses. **l.11 chaplet:** coronet.
l.14 twining in: entwining. **l.16 wreaths:** coils. **l.22 curious frame:**
elaborate design.

p.8 *Eyes and Tears* **l.23 showers:** a noun, with 'is' implied.
l.35 Cynthia teeming: the full moon pouring out her light.

p.10 *Bermudas* **l.1 ride:** like an anchored ship. **l.7 so long
unknown:** the Bermudas were not colonised until 1612. **l.20 Ormus:**
Hormuz, a trading city at the mouth of the Persian Gulf. **l.23 apples
plants:** plants pineapples. **l.28 ambergris:** secretion from sperm whales
found floating in tropical seas and used to make perfume.

p.11 *Clorinda and Damon* **l.5 aim:** intend. **l.8 vade:** 'fade', but
also 'depart'. **l.23 oat:** flute.

p.13 *A Dialogue between the Soul and Body* **l.15 needless:** not
needing anything. **l.29 port:** death.

p.14 *The Nymph Complaining for the Death of her Fawn*
l.17 deodands: things forfeited because they caused a human death.
l.106 turtles: turtledoves.

p.17 *Young Love* **l.9 stay:** wait for. **l.24 prevent:** anticipate.

p.19 *To his Coy Mistress* **coy mistress:** reluctant mistress of his
heart. **l.10 conversion of the Jews:** one of the signs of the Last Judgement.

l.29 quaint honour: fastidious chastity. **l.40 slow-chapped:** slowly devouring. **l.44 Thorough:** through.

p.20 *The Unfortunate Lover* l.36 bill: peck. **ll.43–4 play/At sharp:** fight with unblunted swords. **l.55 'says:** assays, tries. **l.57 banneret:** soldier knighted on the battlefield. **l.64 field . . . gules:** heraldic device of a crimson lover on a black background.

p.22 *The Gallery* l.11 Examining: testing. **l.48 or [Whitehall's] or [Mantua's]:** either . . . or. **l.48 Mantua:** Charles I had bought paintings owned by Vincenzo Gonzaga, Duke of Mantua.

p.24 *The Fair Singer* l.18 gainèd both the wind and sun: in a sea-battle it is advantageous to have wind and sun at the back.

p.25 *Mourning* l.3 infants: tiny relections of one who looks into the eyes of another. **l.29 wide:** inaccurately, wide of the mark.

p.26 *Daphnis and Chloe* l.10 niceness: scrupulousness. **l.12 comprised:** included. **l.83 seed:** ferns (which have no seeds) were thought to have invisible seeds that could make their possessor invisible. **l.107 laws:** laws of nature.

p.31 *The Definition of Love* l.14 close: come together. **l.24 planisphere:** astrolabe. **l.31 conjunction:** in astrology, the appearance of two planets in the same longitude. **l.32 opposition:** in astrology, the appearance of two planets 180° apart (hence 'star-crossed').

p.32 *The Picture of Little T. C. in a Prospect of Flowers* 'T. C.' may be Theophilia Cornewall, in the which case 'darling of the gods' renders the meaning of her name in Greek. **l.17 in time compound:** settle the matter in good time.

p.33 *The Match* l.19 magazine: arsenal.

p.35 *The Mower against Gardens* l.1 Luxurious, in use: voluptuous, into practice. **l.15 root, hold:** bulb, value. **l.18 Marvel of Peru:** a multicoloured tropical plant (*Mirabilis Jalapa*, or four o'clock). **l.35 fauns:** rural gods.

p.36 *Damon the Mower* l.18 Dog Star: the dog-days, the hottest part of the year, were dated with reference to the helical rising of Sirius, the brightest star in the sky. **l.28 gelid:** frozen. **l.54 closes:** fields enclosed with hedges. **l.64 ring:** fairy ring, a circle of grass, the contrasting colour of which is actually caused by fungi. **l.83 shepherd's-purse, and clown's-all-heal:** both *capsella bursa pastoris* and *stachys palustris* were used to stop bleeding.

p.39 *The Mower to the Glow-worms* **l.9 officious:** attentive. **l.12 foolish fires:** will-o'-the-wisp (spontaneously-ignited marsh methane).

p.40 *The Mower's Song* **l.19 ought:** owe.

p.41 *Ametas and Thestylis Making Hay-ropes* **Hay-ropes:** ropes of twisted hay made to bind trusses of hay.

p.42 *Music's Empire* **l.18 solemn noise:** sacred sound.

p.43 *The Garden* **l.5 vergèd shade:** deflected shadow. **l.37 curious:** attractive. **l.41 pleasures less:** lesser pleasures. **l.44 straight:** straight away. **l.51 vest:** vestment, clothing. **l.54 whets:** preens. **l.61 share:** lot. **l.66 dial:** sun-dial.

p.46 *An Horatian Ode upon Cromwell's Return from Ireland* Oliver Cromwell returned from his Irish campaign in May 1650. An Horatian ode is a poem on the model of the Roman poet Horace, in which the first stanza establishes a metrical pattern which is duplicated in subsequent stanzas; Keats's 'Ode to a Nightingale' is another example of the genre. **l.1 forward, appear:** eager, appear in public. **l.4 numbers languishing:** love poems. **l.20 more:** worse. **l.32 bergamot:** a pear associated with royalty (through its derivation from *beg armudi*, prince's pear). **l.42 penetration:** simultaneous occupation of the same space by two bodies. **l.47 Hampton:** Charles fled from Hampton Court Palace on 11 November 1647. **l.52 Carisbrooke:** castle on the Isle of Wight where Charles was imprisoned. **l.60 try:** put to the test. **ll.67–72:** an elaboration of an ancient story in which the discovery of an undamaged head by the builders of the Capitol in Rome was interpreted as an omen of Rome's destiny as a world capital. **l.82 still:** always. **l.86 first year's rents:** annates: the first year's revenue of an ecclesiastical benefice had to be paid to the government. **l.104 climactéric:** precipitating a critical change in life. **l.105 Pict:** Cromwell was planning to invade Scotland in July. **l.107 sad:** steadfast.

p.49 *Upon the Hill and Grove at Bilbrough* Bilbrough: a manor-house near York owned by the Fairfax family. **l.4 like:** even. **l.5 pencil:** paintbrush. **l.9 unjust:** jagged. **l.14 centre:** centre of the earth. **l.28 Tenerife:** mountain of 12,200 feet in the Canary Islands, then believed to be the highest mountain in the world; Bilbrough Hill is 145 feet high. **l.43 Vera:** Fairfax's wife Anne was the daughter of Sir Horace Vere. **l.73 ye trees:** refers to the oaks of Dordona, site of an oracle in ancient Greece.

p.52 *Upon Appleton House* Appleton House, the manor house of Nun Appleton, a former Cistercian priory south of York; when Thomas, Lord Fairfax retired there in 1650 the house was still under construction in the former nunnery. **l.6 vault:** arch. **l.12 equal:** equal to their needs. **l.24 first builders:** builders of the Tower of Babel. **l.30 loop:** opening, loop-hole. **l.36 Vere:** Anne, Lady Fairfax, was the daughter of Sir Horace Vere. **l.64 invent:** discover. **l.73 Bishop's Hill:** (now Bishophill House) was Fairfax's residence in York; Denton was another Fairfax property in Yorkshire (near Ilkley). **l.90 Thwaites:** Isabella Thwaites, General Fairfax's great-great-grandmother, who had been incarcerated in the priory by her aunt, the prioress, in an unsuccessful attempt to prevent her from marrying William Fairfax. **l.105 armour white:** the Cistercian habit. **l.122 legend:** saint's life. **l.152 devoto:** devotee. **l.169 nice:** scrupulous. **l.180 sea-borne amber:** ambergris, a secretion from sperm whales found floating in tropical seas and used to make perfume. **l.181 grieved, pastes:** injured, pastries. **l.182 baits:** refreshments. **l.221 'state:** property. **l.232 from a judge, then soldier:** William Fairfax's father, also William, was a judge in the Court of Common Pleas; his mother was the daughter of Lord Roos, a distinguished soldier who had died at the siege of Tournay. **l.233 storm:** the storming of the nunnery. **l.241 offspring:** Sir Thomas, son of William and Isabella, fought in the Netherlands (one of the Germanies, because Dutch was thought to be a dialect of German); his son Thomas, the first Baron Fairfax, fought in France and Germany, and two of his sons died in the siege of Frankenthal (Germany); Ferdinando, the second Baron, fought in the civil wars of the 1640s; one or more members of the family may have fought with Gustavus Adolphus in Poland. **l.253 disjointed:** distracted. **ll.273–4:** Nun Appleton surrendered after the Act of Dissolution of 1539, and passed as forfeited land (escheat) to Henry VIII and thence to the Fairfax family. **l.281 hero:** either Sir Thomas Fairfax, son of William and Isabella, or his son Baron Fairfax. **l.292 dian:** reveille. **l.295 pan:** part of the musket that contains the priming. **l.301 nymph:** Mary Fairfax, of whom Marvell was tutor. **l.336 Swit-**

zers: the Papal Swiss Guard then, as now, wore striped yellow and red uniforms. **l.341 stoves:** hothouses for plants. **l.349 Cinque Ports:** five ports on the south-east coast of England. **l.351 spanned:** limited. **l.363 Cawood:** a residence (two miles from Nun Appleton) of the Archbishop of York until 1642. **l.385 scene:** no stage that changes scenes with elaborate machinery. **l.395 rail:** the corncrake (or landrail), which nests in fields. **l.395 cates:** food. **l.416 sourdine:** mute. **l.428 Alexander's sweat:** Alexander the Great was reputed to sweat aromatically. **l.439 Roman . . . rise:** construct burial mounds (which were thought to be Roman rather than neolithic). **l.444 cloths for Lely:** canvases for the portrait painter Sir Peter Lely. **l.446 table rase:** blank tablet (*tabula rasa*). **ll.447–8 toril . . . at Madril:** bullring at Madrid. **l.456 D'Avenant . . .** William D'Avenant describes in *Gondibert* the appearance of a 'universal herd' in a painting of the creation. **l.461 Such:** so. **l.480 pound:** cattle pen. **l.486 pressed:** commandeered. **l.502 fifth element:** 'quintessence', the heavenly element. **l.532 throstle:** song-thrush. **l.537 hewel:** green woodpecker. **l.538 holtfelster's care:** woodcutter's responsibility. **l.580 all the plumes:** Cortes reported that the walls of Montezuma's palaces at Tenochtitlan were hung with featherwork. **l.586:** could provide me with clothing appropriate to my studies. **l.599 shed:** part. **l.636 slick:** smooth. **l.649 quills:** fishing floats. **l.650 angles:** fishing rods and lines. **l.659 whished:** hushed. **l.660 bonne mine:** French: good appearance; *bonne* is disyllabic. **l.668 eben shuts:** shutters as black as ebony. **l.669 halcyon:** kingfisher. **l.675 compacts:** solidifies. **l.677 stupid:** stupefied. **ll.679 assist:** attend. **l.684 star new-slain:** meteor. **l.688 vitrified:** transformed into glass (like the crystalline heaven of Ptolemaic astronomy). **ll.713–14 prevent / Those trains:** anticipate that artillery. **l.734 black-bag:** mask. **l.755 Aranjuez:** Spanish royal palace at which Philip II laid out the Jardín de la Isla (later the setting of Schiller's *Don Carlos*). **l.756 Bel-Retiro:** Buen Retiro, another Spanish royal palace with famous gardens. **l.757 Idalian grove:** Mount Ida, near Troy, where Aeneas was conceived through the 'wanton love' of Anchises and Aphrodite. **l.772:** leather-covered coracles were carried by fishermen on their heads.

p.76 The First Anniversary of the Government under His Highness the Lord Protector, 1665 l.68 Instrument: the instrument of the Government which established the Protectorate in 1653. **l.113 whore:** biblical Whore of Babylon, which was identified with the Roman Catholic Church. **l.305 Feake and Simpson:** Fifth Monarchist leaders who had been imprisoned for preaching seditiously against Cromwell.

p.88 *A Poem upon the Death of His Late Highness the Lord Protector*
Oliver Cromwell died on 3 September 1658. **l.21 'signed:** assigned as his
executors. **l.30 Eliza:** Elizabeth Claypole, Cromwell's second daughter,
had died on 6 August 1658. **l.62 feigns:** conceals. **l.67 purple:** echoes
the story of Nisus, who died when his locks were shorn by his daughter
Scylla. **ll.79–80:** the trumpeting of mute swans was interpreted as an omen
of death; kingfishers (halcyons) move to the coast in winter, and were
believed to calm part of the sea in order to nest; the pelican was believed to
feed its young with blood from its own breast. **l.139 cast:** calculate
astrologically. **ll.142–6:** Cromwell died on the anniversary of his victories
at Dunbar (1650) and Worcester (1651). **l.154 Ligny:** the Prince de
Ligne, who had just after Cromwell's death led a force of Spanish soldiers in
an unsuccessful attempt to relieve Ypres. **l.173:** Dunkirk was ceded to
England after the Battle of the Dunes. **l.174:** Cromwell's 'Western Design'
of 1654 was a plan to overturn Spanish control of the West Indies; in 1655
English forces captured Jamaica. **l.178 Confessor:** King Edward the
Confessor, canonised in 1161. **l.187 Preston:** In 1648 Cromwell had
defeated the Scots at Preston. **l.188 Clonmel:** Irish forces successfully
resisted Cromwell's attempt to storm Clonmel in 1650, and then escaped
before the town was surrendered. **l.189 Fenwick:** Colonel Roger Fenwick, who died in the Battle of the Dunes. **ll.201–2:** Richard Williams (later
Sir Richard Cromwell), Oliver Cromwell's great-grandfather, had adopted
the surname of his friend and uncle Sir Thomas Cromwell (later Earl of
Essex). **l.234 Janus' double gate:** the *Janus geminus* in the Forum in
Rome; the closing of the gates signified peace. **l.245 Francisca:** Frances
Rich, Cromwell's youngest daughter. **l.259 feign:** imagine. **l.287 pitch:**
the height from which a falcon swoops. **l.305 Richard:** Cromwell's son
Richard was proclaimed Protector on the day of his father's death.
l.317 enchased: adorned

p.95 *Flecknoe, an English Priest at Rome* Marvell visited the priest,
poet, musician and dramatist Richard Flecknoe in Rome during Lent of
1648 or 1649. **l.4 Lord Brooke:** Fulke Greville, to whose *Remains*
Flecknoe was to contribute commendatory verses in 1670. **l.6 Sad
Pelican:** an emblem of the redemptive sacrifice of Jesus, because the pelican
was believed to feed her young with blood taken from her own breast. **l.12:**
neither black hangings nor winding sheets. **l.18 stanzas:** 'stanza' plays on
the Italian sense of 'room'; the seventeenth-century spelling of 'apartment'
preserves the fourth syllable. **l.55 scant:** fasting. **l.63 *basso rilievo*:**
(Italian) low-relief sculpture. **l.74 *sottana*:** cassock (soutane). **l.76 first
Council of Antioch:** convened in AD 264. **l.90 thorough:** through.

l.98 delightful: delighted. **l.99 penetration:** simultaneous occupation of the same space by two bodies. **ll.100–1:** Reference to doctrine of the Trinity, which holds that the Godhead consists of three persons in one substance. **l.120 Assizes:** circuit court for trying civil and criminal cases. **l.126:** Suetonius records that no one was allowed to leave the theatre during Nero's recital. **l.130 foul copies:** rough drafts. **l.136 ordinaries:** public eating-houses. **l.137 chancres and poulains:** syphilitic ulcers and sores. **l.152 Perillus:** an Athenian artist who designed a hollow bronze bull designed to roast criminals alive and elicit cries like the roaring of a bull; he presented the bull to the Sicilian tyrant Phaleris, who made Perillus its first victim.

p.100 *To his Noble Friend Mr Richard Lovelace upon his Poems* Marvell's commendatory poem was printed in Lovelace's *Lucasta* in 1649. **l.22 consistory:** court of presbyters. **l.28 privilege:** privilege of free speech in the House of Commons. **l.29 sequestration:** Lovelace's estate was confiscated on 28 November 1648. **l.30:** Lovelace's best-known poem was 'To Lucasta, Going to the Wars'. **ll.31–2:** Lovelace had been imprisoned in 1642 for submitting to Parliament a Kentish petition in support of the king

p.101 *Tom May's Death* The poet, playwright and translator Thomas May died on 13 November 1650. **l.7 The Pope's Head, The Mitre:** taverns in Stephen's Alley, Westminster, where May lived. **l.8 still:** always. **l.10 Ayres:** unidentified, but presumably a tavern-keeper. **l.13 Ben:** Ben Jonson, who had written commendatory verses for May's translation of Lucan's *Pharsalia*. **l.14 layed:** sang a lay. **ll.21–4:** a parody of the opening lines of May's translation of Lucan. **l.37:** In 1634 the Earl of Pembroke had broken his staff of office (as Lord Chamberlain) on May during a performance of a masque at court; the king ordered Pembroke to apologise and pay restitution. **l.41 Polydore ... Alan:** Polydore Vergil (the early Tudor court historian), the Alani (a tribe that fought for the Huns). **l.50:** The house of the Virgin Mary had been carried by angels from Nazareth (not Bethlehem) to Dalmatia in 1291 and then to Loreto in 1295. **l.53 lay:** sang. **l.54:** May wrote *A Continuation of Lucan's Historical Poem*. **l.57 one:** Sir William D'Avenant, who succeeded Jonson as Poet Laureate. **l.62:** accepts a fee to join one side or the other; in medieval Italy Guelfs were supporters of the papacy, Ghibellines of the empire. **l.82:** the Council of State paid for May's burial in Westminster Abbey. **l.94: vulture** the vulture that ate the perpetually renewing liver of Prometheus

Everyman's Poetry

William Blake
ed. Peter Butter
0 460 87800 X

The Brontës
ed. Pamela Norris
0 460 87864 6

Rupert Brooke & Wilfred Owen
ed. George Walter
0 460 87801 8

Robert Burns
ed. Donald Low
0 460 87814 X

Lord Byron
ed. Jane Stabler
0 460 87810 7

John Clare
ed. R. K. R. Thornton
0 460 87823 9

Samuel Taylor Coleridge
ed. John Beer
0 460 87826 3

Four Metaphysical Poets
ed. Douglas Brooks-Davies
0 460 87857 3

Oliver Goldsmith
ed. Robert L. Mack
0 460 87827 1

Thomas Gray
ed. Robert Mack
0 460 87805 0

Ivor Gurney
ed. George Walter
0 460 87797 6

Heinrich Heine
ed. T. J. Reed & David Cram
0 460 87865 4

George Herbert
ed. D. J. Enright
0 460 87795 X

Robert Herrick
ed. Douglas Brooks-Davies
0 460 87799 2

John Keats
ed. Nicholas Roe
0 460 87808 5

Henry Wadsworth Longfellow
ed. Anthony Thwaite
0 460 87821 2

Andrew Marvell
ed. Gordon Campbell
0 460 87812 3

John Milton
ed. Gordon Campbell
0 460 87813 1

Edgar Allan Poe
ed. Richard Gray
0 460 87804 2

Poetry Please!
Foreword by Charles Causley
0 460 87824 7

Alexander Pope
ed. Douglas Brooks-Davies
0 460 87798 4

Alexander Pushkin
ed. A. D. P. Briggs
0 460 87862 X

Lord Rochester
ed. Paddy Lyons
0 460 87819 0

Christina Rossetti
ed. Jan Marsh
0 460 87820 4

William Shakespeare
ed. Martin Dodsworth
0 460 87815 8

John Skelton
ed. Greg Walker
0 460 87796 8

Alfred, Lord Tennyson
ed. Michael Baron
0 460 87802 6

R. S. Thomas
ed. Anthony Thwaite
0 460 87811 5

Walt Whitman
ed. Ellman Crasnow
0 460 87825 5

Oscar Wilde
ed. Robert Mighall
0 460 87803 4